Stronger Together

For John McKim

on Yom Hashoah

April 30, 2019

THE AZRIELI SERIES OF HOLOCAUST SURVIVOR MEMOIRS: PUBLISHED TITLES

Stronger Together

Ibolya (Szalai) Grossman
and Andy Réti

THE AZRIELI FOUNDATION · www.azrielifoundation.org

Cover and book design by Mark Goldstein
Endpaper maps by Martin Gilbert
Map on page xxvii by François Blanc

LIBRARY AND ARCHIVES CANADA CATALOGUING IN PUBLICATION

Grossman, Ibolya Szalai, 1916–2005, author
    Stronger Together/ Ibolya (Szalai) Grossman and Andy Réti.

(The Azrieli series of Holocaust survivor memoirs)
Includes index.
Contains edited and condensed versions of: An ordinary woman in extraordinary times / Ibolya (Szalai) Grossman; The son of an extraordinary woman/ Andy Réti.
ISBN 978-1-988065-02-1 (paperback) · 8 7 6 5 4 3 2

1. Grossman, Ibolya Szalai, 1916–2005. 2. Holocaust survivors – Hungary – Biography. 3. Hungarians – Canada – Biography. 4. Hungary – Politics and government – 1918–1945. 5. Hungary – Politics and government – 1945–. 6. Hungary – Social conditions. 7. Réti, Andy, 1942-. 8. Jewish refugees – Canada – Biography. 9. Hungarian Canadians – Biography. 10. Children of Holocaust survivors – Canada – Biography. 11. Immigrants – Canada – Biography. I. Réti, Andy, 1942–, author II. Grossman, Ibolya Szalai, 1916-2005. Ordinary woman in extraordinary times. III. Réti, Andy, 1942– . Son of an extraordinary woman. IV. Azrieli Foundation, issuing body V. Title.

DS135.H93A14 2016   940.53'180922439   C2016-902253-6

PRINTED IN CANADA

The Azrieli Series of Holocaust Survivor Memoirs

Naomi Azrieli, Publisher

Jody Spiegel, Program Director
Arielle Berger, Managing Editor
Matt Carrington, Editor
Devora Levin, Assistant Editor
Elizabeth Lasserre, Senior Editor, French-Language Editions
Elin Beaumont, Senior Education Outreach and Program Facilitator
Catherine Person, Bilingual Education and Outreach Coordinator
Stephanie Corazza, Education and Curriculum Associate
Marc-Olivier Cloutier, Bilingual Educational Outreach and Events
    Assistant
Elizabeth Banks, Digital Asset Curator and Archivist
Susan Roitman, Office Manager (Toronto)
Mary Mellas, Executive Assistant and Human Resources (Montreal)

Mark Goldstein, Art Director
François Blanc, Cartographer
Bruno Paradis, Layout, French-Language Editions

Contents

Series Preface:
In their own words. . .

In telling these stories, the writers have liberated themselves. For so many years we did not speak about it, even when we became free people living in a free society. Now, when at last we are writing about what happened to us in this dark period of history, knowing that our stories will be read and live on, it is possible for us to feel truly free. These unique historical documents put a face on what was lost, and allow readers to grasp the enormity of what happened to six million Jews – one story at a time.

David J. Azrieli, C.M., C.Q., M.Arch
Holocaust survivor and founder, The Azrieli Foundation

Since the end of World War II, approximately 40,000 Jewish Holocaust survivors have immigrated to Canada. Who they are, where they came from, what they experienced and how they built new lives for themselves and their families are important parts of our Canadian heritage. The Azrieli Foundation's Holocaust Survivor Memoirs Program was established in 2005 to preserve and share the memoirs written by those who survived the twentieth-century Nazi genocide of the Jews of Europe and later made their way to Canada. The program is guided by the conviction that each survivor of the Holocaust has a remarkable story to tell, and that such stories play an important role in education about tolerance and diversity.

Millions of individual stories are lost to us forever. By preserving the stories written by survivors and making them widely available to a broad audience, the Azrieli Foundation's Holocaust Survivor Memoirs Program seeks to sustain the memory of all those who perished at the hands of hatred, abetted by indifference and apathy. The personal accounts of those who survived against all odds are as different as the people who wrote them, but all demonstrate the courage, strength, wit and luck that it took to prevail and survive in such terrible adversity. The memoirs are also moving tributes to people – strangers and friends – who risked their lives to help others, and who, through acts of kindness and decency in the darkest of moments, frequently helped the persecuted maintain faith in humanity and courage to endure. These accounts offer inspiration to all, as does the survivors' desire to share their experiences so that new generations can learn from them.

The Holocaust Survivor Memoirs Program collects, archives and publishes these distinctive records and the print editions are available free of charge to educational institutions and Holocaust-education programs across Canada. They are also available for sale to the general public at bookstores. All revenues to the Azrieli Foundation from the sales of the Azrieli Series of Holocaust Survivor Memoirs go toward the publishing and educational work of the memoirs program.

~

The Azrieli Foundation would like to express appreciation to the following people for their invaluable efforts in producing this book: Doris Bergen, Sherry Dodson (Maracle Press), Barbara Kamieński, Karen Kligman, Therese Parent, and Margie Wolfe & Emma Rodgers of Second Story Press.

About the Glossary

The following memoir contains a number of terms, concepts and historical references that may be unfamiliar to the reader. For information on major organizations; significant historical events and people; geographical locations; religious and cultural terms; and foreign-language words and expressions that will help give context and background to the events described in the text, please see the glossary beginning on page 217.

Introduction

"A true story with happiness and sadness in it."[1]

Soon after I read Ibolya Grossman's memoir, first published in 1990 as *An Ordinary Woman in Extraordinary Times*, I worked up the courage to call her. On the other end of the telephone line was a modest and welcoming voice. The family consisted of two survivors – Ibi and her son, Andy – whose love for each other eclipsed any solely academic interest I might once have had in the genre of the memoir, the period of the war in Budapest and its environs, and the narration of two memoirs of the Holocaust. With Ibi's encouragement, I came to understand my need to try to make sense of the crime of the rapid decimation of Hungary's Jews and Roma, and I reflected on what has become a method of "understanding" now: the act of retracing steps – in this case, Ibi's and Andy's – through the Jewish quarter of Budapest, the former ghetto area in Pest and, eventually, the house in which they were forced to live in the Budapest ghetto until they were liberated by Soviet forces in the yard at Akácfa [Acacia] Street. In other words, it was my own romantic view of Hungary as homeland

---

1 Ibi Grossman, "January 1987, To my son" in *The Son of an Extraordinary Woman*. Introduction Marlene Kadar. (Toronto: A M A G raphics, 2002), 3.

that was challenged, and as I struggled to speak my father's first language, Ibi and Andy aimed only to speak mine.

In the long aftermath of World War II, Europe's economic losses worsened: pre-war populations suffered great civilian losses; enormous military casualties; the bombardment of grand cities, the distinctive Danube bridges and multiform architecture – from Gothic to Art-Nouveau, Roman to Bauhaus, and Turkish styles to an array of synagogue architectures; and the continuing tragic devastation of Europe's Jewish population in real numbers and in forced migrations abroad. Nowhere were these losses more palpable than in Hungary and, tragically, in the absolute final stages of the war. There, not only had the majority of Hungarian Jewry been murdered, but also its smaller Roma population, murdered in the Gypsy family camps or scattered across Europe. Hungary was an "independent" ally of Nazi Germany until March 19, 1944, the day Germany occupied Hungary. On April 5, Jews were forced to wear the yellow star. One month later, in May, mass deportations began. "Between May 15 and July 9, 1944, 437,402 Jews were deported from Hungary."[2] The Canadian survivor Rudolf Vrba, born in Slovakia, co-author of the renowned Vrba-Wetzler report, attested to the organization of the murder of the Hungarians who would be arriving in Auschwitz from Hungary in 1944, a selection that did not, by chance, include Ibi and Andy. Vrba affirms that fewer than 5 per cent of the Hungarian deportees returned.[3]

Prior to the deportations, approximately 825,000 Jews lived in

---

2 Dieter Vaupel, "The Hessisch Lichtenau Sub-camp of the Buchenwald Concentration Camp, 1944–45," in *Studies on the Holocaust in Hungary*, ed. Randolph L. Braham (Boulder, CO: Social Science Monographs; New York: Csengeri Institute for Holocaust Studies of the Graduate School and University Center of the CUNY, 1990), 199.

3 Rudolf Vrba, "The Preparations for the Holocaust in Hungary: An Eyewitness Account," in *The Nazis' Last Victims: The Holocaust in Hungary*, eds. Randolph Braham and Scott Miller (Detroit: Wayne State University Press, 1998).

Hungary; according to the 1941 census, 200,000 of these resided in Budapest proper. The Jews in Budapest were not subjected to the same en masse deportations as those residing throughout the rest of the country – they were, instead, harassed and restricted by several anti-Jewish laws; and in October 1944, at the mercy of a new fascist regime led by the Arrow Cross Party, Jews were increasingly rounded up, assaulted and murdered. On October 15, 1944, Hungary's Regent, Admiral Miklós Horthy, had announced that Hungary was not going to war, and that "nobody had to worry." Ibi thought this meant she could tear the yellow star off her chest. But later that day, Ferencz Szálasi and the Arrow Cross Party took over the government, intent on collaborating with the Nazis and murdering the Jewish population who remained in Budapest. In November 1944, Ibi and Andy were among thousands incarcerated in the Budapest ghetto. But they held on long enough that they were saved from deportation and death, protected by the Russians who freed them and then by the Allies who followed close on their heels.

Ibolya Szalai Grossman was an ordinary woman who lived through extraordinary times with grace, verve and joyfulness whenever possible. This she did without ignoring the past, her past, and a life that included the death of her loved ones, especially Zoltán, her husband and the father of her only child, Andy Réti. My pressing curiosity about Andy Réti and his beloved mother, Ibi, actually began in a symbolic reading of the "writing" of Andy's absent father – a man of course impossible for me to have met in real life. But I came to know him because his memory behaved as a muse, not just to me, but also to both Ibi and Andy.

Zoltán Rechnitzer was murdered by the Third Reich months before the end of the war. His death was tragic in the same way all deaths are, but also because if only he had lived for just a few more months, he would have experienced the same "liberation" that befell the rest of his young family. It is no surprise that this sense of regret permeates both memoirs. In January 1987, prior to the publication of

An Ordinary Woman in Extraordinary Times, Ibi wrote to her son, "What a wonderful and loving father my husband would have been. If only he had lived." Andy's memoir honours this sentiment.

Zoltán was, sadly, one of at least 42,000 Hungarian Jewish forced labourers who died before liberation, largely in the Ukraine and other neighbouring countries. The Labour Service, first implemented in Hungary in 1939, became increasingly focused on persecuting Jews as "unreliable elements."[4] "At its height, there were 80,000 workers in this program, many of whom worked side by side with German soldiers at the front."[5] On November 25, 1942, a notice posted in Budapest read: "All Jewish men between the ages of 18 and 50 must report to army headquarters for service." Zoltán reported for army duty and was given a Hungarian soldier's army cap but no uniform. He was unarmed and wore a yellow armband. Soldiers who were half-Jewish wore white armbands. Zoltán was taken to the Felvidék in northern Hungary, now part of Slovakia. Conditions of forced labour were brutal, yet somehow, in the midst of it, Zoltán was able to send sixteen postcards to his wife; the most significant one, the ninth, entreated her to take notes on the events for the sake of historical memory. In code from some unknown location in some unidentified forced labour camp, he wrote in a communiqué permitted by the censors, "Write down everything just as you know it."

Everything that Ibi knows is not contained here in her memoir, nor is everything Andy knows. But Zoltán wanted to impart some special status to the verb "to know," as though he himself realized that knowing the facts, never mind the truth of his own circumstance, was an impossibility under the current regime. Of the sixteen postcards to Ibi – written in code when possible – the ninth is the one

---

4 Randolph Braham, "The Holocaust in Hungary: A Retrospective Analysis" in *The Nazis' Last Victims: The Holocaust in Hungary.* 34.

5 Dieter Vaupel, "The Hessisch Lichtenau Sub-camp of the Buchenwald Concentration Camp, 1944–45," 199.

that caught my attention. It never occurred to me then that I, too, would enter into an unending conversation with Zoltán and his family. For me, Zoltán is a powerful force that set the stage for his family to become writers when he wrote what have become prophetic words. If we stretch our minds just a little bit, we can imagine that in that card Zoltán set the stage for both Ibi and Andy to write these two memoirs.

I came to know Andy and his story because I pursued Ibi and hers. In Ibi's memoir we have the narration of older memories in Hungary, first with her immediate family in the more southern section of the country, Pécs, and then in Budapest where she lived with Zoltán and her in-laws until her exodus. Andy's memoir expounds on this history, filling in some of the gaps in family life that evolved and changed in Canada once Andy and Ibi were settled, and as Andy began his own family.

Andy's experience of the Holocaust is less vivid than Ibi's, and sometimes second-hand, because he was just a child during wartime. But his life was affected and his memories do scar his continuing willingness to rehabilitate his homeland in his mind and heart. Even so, the majority of his more detailed remembered past hails from immigration, life in Winnipeg and then Toronto, and the new family he established here.

Andy's story is a version of Ibi's story, told from the point of view of an adult remembering the Holocaust and immigration to Canada from the child's point of view. During the writing, he does become the adult he is today. Both stories are a continuing attempt – made palpable again today with the republication of their memoirs in a new version where the books are companion pieces[6] – to carry

---

6 The Azrieli Series of Holocaust Survivor Memoirs has published a number of companion pieces in the period leading up to the inevitable Ibi-Andy companion piece. This is the first mother-son combination, which is uniquely situated in the history of remembrance as the stories both intersect and diverge, and

on the loving conversation with the man Andy called "Daddy Zolti." Andy's memoir also stands as its own testimony and as a tribute to his mother's life.

In lieu of Zoltán's presence during his childhood, Andy was able to substitute his paternal grandfather, a man who, however, did not attend his bar mitzvah. Andy's wisdom allows him to remember that, "if something wasn't important for [his grandfather], then it wasn't important for me either. The connection between my father's murder and our Judaism did not occur to me until later in my life." Most telling is the extreme sign of his grandfather's pure love for his grandson. As Andy writes, "He loved me, so he let me go" – in other words, he let Andy and his mother proceed with their escape to the west on the M.S. *Berlin* a few days after Christmas in the year of the revolutionary events of 1956. How final this sailing must have seemed at the time; how final, in fact, it became.

Ibi had explained to her son, in order to persuade him to join her in a second attempt to escape her homeland:

During the war, you were only two years old. We were lucky to be taken to the ghetto, even though many of us died of hunger and sickness or by shooting. You were near death because you were very ill and there was

---

one expands or comments on the other. As such, readers witness the collective triumph of the first-person narrator. Women survivors have taken their rightful place in this method of publication because they retain their roles as companions themselves, as ones who love and care for others in this practice – though of course they can break out of this mold and achieve something separately. The other companion pieces in the Azrieli Series of Holocaust Survivor Memoirs, also unique among memoirs are: husband and wife Rachel & Adam Shtibel (*The Violin/ A Child's Testimony*, 2007); father and daughter William Tannenzapf & Renate Krakauer (*Memories From the Abyss/ But I Had a Happy Childhood*, 2009); the parallel stories of Judy Abrams & Eva Felsenburg Marx (*Tenuous Threads/ One of the Lucky Ones*, 2011); and husband and wife Bronia & Joseph Beker (*Joy Runs Deeper*, 2014).

no doctor, no medicine and no food. And all those things happened to us because we are Jews. You also know that is the reason your daddy was killed. Right now, we are in the midst of a revolution, and I don't want the same thing to happen to us again. Now we have our chance to escape and to start a new and peaceful life somewhere else.

In spite of Ibi and Andy's obvious gratitude at being able to escape their circumstance and move to Canada, Ibi still reflects on the adjustment. Her reflection does not exclude the possibility that "happiness" is not a simple word, and that a life marked by scars and traumatic memories always straddles the constant balance between joy and regret. She writes, "Although I had difficulties in adjusting to my new life in the first few months, I was in high spirits. Sometimes, when I think back on those days, I feel that I was happier than I was many years later, when I had my own bungalow. I'm not sure if I can explain why that was, but perhaps it had something to do with the circumstances I had left in Hungary, where I never had my own home and I was dependent on my in-laws." Both sadness and happiness mix ambiguously in Ibi's denouement – often so sublimely described in the recent past by literary writers such as W. G. Sebald, Bernhard Schlink and the remarkable Nobel Prize winner Patrick Modiano.

Ibi's narration of migration and life in Canada is not romanticized – certainly she and Andy found it difficult to adjust to temperatures that hovered at −40° when they disembarked the train in Winnipeg. But, most importantly, there are also incidents of racism and antisemitism in the new land that puncture Ibi's generally positive view of her new life. These disturb her most when they affect her little boy, as happened in Winnipeg when he got into a fight with a boy who called him "stinky Jew." The good news was, Andy reported, that the boy had more bruises than he did.

As sanguine as Andy may have felt in Winnipeg, life sweetened in Toronto. Punctuated by normal growing pains, Andy writes clearly and movingly about Bloor Street and Spadina Avenue and where they intersect at the "Jewish Y." This is where he found all his friends, where he was reunited with former classmates from the homeland, lovingly recalled as the "Hungarian" contingent of the "Y."

A recurring theme of both memoirs, and of other memoirs in the Azrieli Series, is that of community. The motif of gathering and re-gathering until some new relationship to the host culture is achieved, and a new level of learning brings a modicum of peace. For both mother and son, learning is the most important aspect of the life well lived, whether it be formal or casual, as we witness in Andy's claim to a "self-awarded PhD." Learning is something that takes place within the community as much as it takes place in the university and else-where. It is this belief that inspired both mother and son to become docents and public speakers, lest we forget.

Most memories about the Holocaust are full of grief and loss in the end, but each one configures that grief and loss in a particular way. What we appreciate as readers are the variety of ways human be-ings appear to "manage," or not manage, as the case may be, and with-out judgment, we read on. The challenge of conquering the event and then the emotions that arise as a consequence of the event is a more convincing response to the sense of loss. Of course conquering grief and loss is an ethos readers prefer to find when they reach the end of a sad or melancholy story. This is what we learn from archetypal critics such as Northrop Frye, but neither fiction nor non-fictional memoirs abide such prescriptions: in fact the real life of Hungary's Jewry can rarely conform to this plot-story. Readers are not always fully cognizant of the harm done to survivors, sometimes unable to fathom the level of horror, but they don't always realize that they, too, use the rather distant suffering of others to amend their own memo-ries or massage their own sorrows, sometimes extremely complicated guilt and shame, often simply the sorrow that only sincere empathy can bring. Readers can fulfill the role of witnesses for memoirists, witnesses who were not there at the time of the invasion and the in-carcerations (and never could be), the deportations and the murders.

But they are witnesses nonetheless,[7] now to the loss survivors encountered in the past and must, of existential necessity, document in the present; they are witnesses to the grief, of more than seventy years ago, that persists into the twenty-first century. Who can sustain a loss for more than seventy years without cracks showing bare and scars opening and closing as if to the sounds of alarm bells? Some scars may be represented with subtlety, some not.

Andy has a way of finding the cracks through which memory is filtered just enough to be sweet, purposeful. A good example is the articulation of his reunion with his "beloved grandparents" in 1963 for a celebration of their golden anniversary. It is in the chapter about this reunion that Andy's memoir underlines two oft-repeated lessons: first, that his mother raised him "by setting some very high standards," by which she lived herself; and second: the Holocaust, or the Shoah, is never replaced by pure joy or by ignorance. The golden anniversary, for example, celebrates the love of the grandparents, but it is also an occasion to "never forget": it was "exactly eighteen years after the Shoah," Andy writes.

Mixed in with these lessons is also the directive to take care of others, to prevent any further abuse of human rights or the denial of dignity. Witness "three physical confrontations" during Andy's career as a taxi-driver, none of which he appears to regret in spite of the potential to threaten the safety of his new young family. One gets the sense from this family that what is right is simply right, and must be acted upon with ardour.

~

---

7 There is a burgeoning, sophisticated literature on the work that witnessing does even as new generations birth new questions. See Marlene Kadar, *Women and Work in World War II* (Waterloo: Wilfrid Laurier University Press, 2015) and Dori Laub, *Testimony: Crises of Witnessing in Literature, Psychoanalysis and History* (New York: Routledge, 1991).

Ibi Grossman's contribution to our present-day world has to do with four elements: first, she survived numerous attempts on her life in her home country, Hungary; second, she withstood horrendous mental and physical suffering during the Holocaust in Hungary, especially between 1942 and 1944, and during her escape to the West; third, she overcame the obstacles faced by all central European Jewish immigrants and made a new home in Canada in a new language and a new, predominantly Christian culture; and fourth, she did all of this after her husband, her parents and two of her sisters died in death camps during the implementation of the Final Solution program in Hungary, leaving her to raise a baby boy alone.[8]

Ibi's story attests to her success in assimilating and, in turn, documents a significant moment in Hungarian Holocaust history and the consequent history of the migration of Hungarians to Canada. The immigration of more than thirty thousand Jewish refugees from Europe constitutes a particular moment in Canada's migration histories – these refugees helped develop the Canadian economy and contributed to significant other features of a younger nation.

Ibolya's life stands now as a symbol of human dignity, intelligence and forbearance, as does Andy's. In her footsteps the son continues the original project his father set out for his mother: write down everything that you know about the historical period in which we have lost our homeland, our friends, our families but not our dignity. Death did not separate Ibi from Zoltán's love just as death did not separate Andy from Ibi's. It is no surprise that Andy began the publication of his own 2002 memoir, *The Son of an Extraordinary Woman*, with the 1987 letter Ibi wrote to him. It once again invokes the memory of Zoltán and links it to the fact, the act of writing itself: "I would like to tell you a little

---

8   A chronology of Ibi's life can be found in Marlene Kadar, "'Write Down Everything Just as You Know It': A Portrait of Ibolya Szalai Grossman," in *Great Dames*, eds. Elspeth Cameron and Janice Dickin (Toronto: University of Toronto Press, 1997), 21–34.

bit about your father, whom you don't remember. You were just a baby when the Nazis took him away to a labour camp and he was killed later on. So read, my son, I'll write you a true story with happiness and sadness in it."

The rare event of a combined memoir sets the bar high, committing to memory a tiny segment of the history of the destruction of Hungarian Jewry. At the same time, it ensures that a coherent familial voice stands watch against prejudice, denial and the erosion of rights in the host country while enshrining an important account of the Holocaust in Hungary and the sometimes conflicted post-1956 migration to our own country. As Andy says in his memoir, "two books, one message."

∽

In memory of Rishma Dunlop (1956–2016) who writes to her daughter in the poem "Postscript",
"My bruises … pale beside the wounds of history."[9]

Marlene Kadar
2016

---

9 "Postscript" in *Lover Through Departure: New and Selected Poems* (Toronto: Mansfield, 2011), 140.

The ninth postcard that Zoltán wrote to Ibolya, which reads, *My dear little heart, Since I had to travel here and there in the past while, I couldn't write to tell you how much I love you and that I can hardly wait to see you again; the time since I last saw you feels like an eternity to me. What is our little Andris [Andy] doing and <u>write down everything just as you know it.</u> You don't need to worry about me, I'm taking care of myself and I will do anything to get home as soon as I can. I hope there is nothing the matter with you, I am thinking of you and my little Andris all the time. I kiss you and Andris many many times. Zolti*

Map

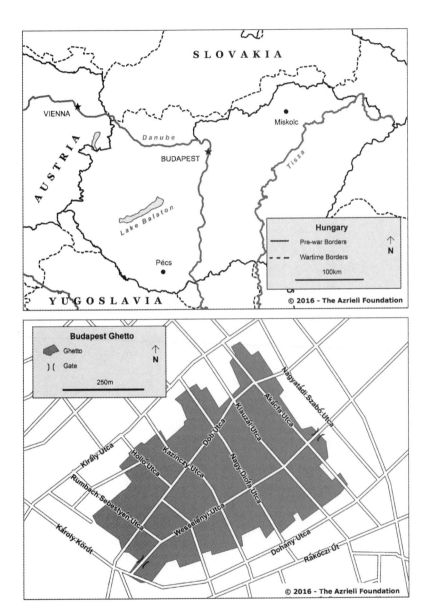

Ibolya Grossman

To the memory of my parents, Ignácz and Laura Szalai, who were killed by the Nazis in 1944.

I wrote my life story at the request of my son, Andy, and I dedicate it to him, his wife, Magdi, and my two beloved grandchildren, David and Kati. I finished writing my life story at the beginning of 1990. I pray and hope that the good Lord will give me some more years in good health so that I will be able to see my grandchildren grow to be decent Canadian citizens with professions of their own liking and choosing.

I would like to express my gratitude to my creative writing teachers, Barbara Turner, Maria Gould and Jayne Brinklow, who helped and encouraged me to write stories about my past, which I later compiled to form a memoir. As a person writing in my second language, I often doubted if I could write my story. On one occasion, Jayne Brinklow wrote on one of my efforts, "Do not be discouraged by the red marks! This is the icing only…. You have baked a lovely cake!"

Prologue

For some strange reason, I still use the old, tattered Hungarian-English dictionary that I bought in Winnipeg in the summer of 1957. I remember that summer day very well. I got off the bus at the wrong stop and consequently had a long walk to the bookstore in the heat; the temperature was 38°C.

On the first page of the dictionary, I see my son's signature – Réti András, his name in Hungarian – underlined twice to show that the dictionary is his. Under his name is mine, Réti Ibolya, with the family name of my late husband and our first address, 130 Machray Ave., Winnipeg. Under that are two other addresses in Winnipeg and my son's name again, this time in English – Andrew Réti – and the address 301/A Markham St., Toronto. There are four more addresses, including that of our last home.

The dictionary's pages are all loose, every one of them, and so are the brown front and back covers. Most of the pages are torn, and some are barely legible. As I carefully turn the pages, I find an old, yellowed piece of paper cut out of a Hungarian-language newspaper in 1963. It says that we welcome my in-laws, Réti Henrik and his wife, Janka, from Hungary and that they are the first couple from an Iron

Curtain country allowed to visit Canada.[1] It also says that they will celebrate their fiftieth wedding anniversary with us here in Toronto.

Why do I still treasure this piece of paper? And why do I still use this dictionary instead of a new one in better shape? They are mementos – some of the first things I acquired in my new life in Canada. The book became a symbol of freedom to me when I bought it on that hot summer day many years ago. This dictionary has helped me to speak English. It has helped me to write. And I have many things in my mind to write about. As I put them down on paper, I still use my faithful dictionary.

1 For information on the Iron Curtain as well as on other historical, religious and cultural terms; significant historical events and people; geographical locations; major organizations; and foreign-language words and expressions contained in the text, please see the glossary.

Five Sisters

Sunday mornings, when our mother got up but our father was still in bed, my younger sister, Elizabeth, and I, who were four and five years old, would jump into our parents' bed and beg our father, "Please, tell us more stories about your past." My father's name was Ignácz Szalai, and he was a slight man with dark, almost black hair and blue eyes. This contrast, along with his perky moustache, made him very handsome. He was blessed with an optimistic personality. In addition to being good-humoured, he was always ready to help those in need.

I recall some of his stories. One of my favourites took place in 1890, when my father was about eighteen years old and wandering from village to village looking for a job. Father had no money left, so he knocked on a door in a small village and asked for food. Probably he didn't look like a typical beggar, because the little girl who opened the door ran inside, shouting, "Mother, come quickly – there is a gentleman beggar in the doorway."

Another of his stories was so sad that, as a little girl, I cried when I heard it. During World War I, when the two sides were in hand-to-hand combat, Father faced a Russian soldier. Both had bayonets in their hands. My father was a split second faster and stabbed the enemy. But when the Russian soldier fell back he screamed, "Shema Yisrael," which is Hebrew for "Hear, O Israel." Father was shocked. With tears in his eyes, he whispered, "I killed a Jew." But it was war, and he would have been killed if the other soldier had been faster.

When Father got older, he stopped wandering, settled down and got married. Unfortunately, his wife died from an illness after a few years of marriage, and he was left with two little girls, Margaret and Ilona, who were eight and four years old at the time. The only solution was for him to remarry. Soon after his wife's death, he was introduced to a woman in her early thirties, Laura, who was willing to marry him and be a stepmother to his daughters.

After they married in 1911, they moved to the city of Pécs, the capital of the Hungarian province of Baranya, where my father opened a tinsmith shop. They also bought a small family home. My sister Aranka was born soon after, in 1912. There were two more babies after Aranka, a boy and a girl, who both died in infancy. Then, in 1916, I was born, and a year later, my sister Elizabeth.

When I was four and Elizabeth was three, we started kindergarten. The kindergarten was close to our home, so after a little while we went by ourselves, holding each other's hand. I still have some vivid memories of my kindergarten years: colouring papers, braiding little baskets, threading beads for necklaces and playing games.

When the weather permitted, we went out to the yard to play. There were some baby chickens in the yard, yellow, fluffy little things. We were told not to touch them. I would watch them as they ran after their mother and from time to time bent their heads to peck at the ground. How I wished to pick one of them up and pet its tiny body! One day, a terrible thing happened. A boy stepped on one of the chicks, and it died. The boy cried loudly, saying over and over that it had been an accident. For punishment, he was separated from his classmates for the rest of the afternoon and was not allowed to play.

At lunchtime, we all went from the yard to the only schoolroom, which was huge. There was one long, low table, where we worked and drew pictures. Along the wall were benches on which we sat to eat our lunch. All of us had to bring our own lunches. We brought our food in little baskets of different shapes and colours. The teachers would lift each one up, asking, "Whose is this?" When we recognized our own, we went to get it and then returned to the bench to eat. After lunch, we had to line up at the sink to get a drink of water – all from the same enamel cup. Then we went to the washroom in groups, and after that we went back to the benches to have our nap. We each had to put our head on the next child's shoulder and either go to sleep or be quiet and motionless for a period of time. My neck hurt by the time we were allowed to stand up, but I was afraid to complain.

After our nap, some of the children got a slice of black bread. I always wanted a slice, too. At home, we didn't have black bread because Mother baked two big, round, white loaves every week. So, one day, I lined up for the bread with the others. As I took the first bite, I looked up and saw my mother coming toward me. She shook her head in disapproval, took the bread out of my hand and gave it to the child nearest me. I learned much later that despite our poverty, Mother was too proud to receive any charity. Even though we were poor, our parents always provided food for the family.

I remember Mother crying often, although I didn't know why at the time. She had a very difficult time with her two stepdaughters. Before our father's remarriage, everybody had told them that a stepmother was evil. Mother did everything she could to show them that she was not, but nothing helped. My younger stepsister, Ilona, was very much under the influence of Margaret, the older one.

I was four years old when I overheard Margaret saying to Ilona, "Hurry into your room before our ice cream melts so we can eat in peace." I ran to my mother, asking, "Mother, what is ice cream, and why didn't you give me any?" Mother was surprised that Margaret and Ilona hadn't given us younger girls any ice cream, even though she had told them to do so. I wished that my big sisters would give me just a little bite to taste. Because of them, Aranka, Elizabeth and I missed out on many things.

Mother tried to please Margaret and Ilona to demonstrate that she wasn't a bad stepmother. My parents had bought them a piano, borrowing money and going into debt for it. Margaret and Ilona took piano lessons. Sometimes my parents had no money to pay the piano teacher, so Mother gave her some merchandise from our store instead. I loved to listen to that piano music so much! I always asked either Margaret or Ilona to play for us younger girls when we were put to bed.

It is from this period that I recall some early childhood fears of going to sleep. Many times, as I lay in bed, half-asleep, I had the feeling that I was stepping into the room only to face a gaping hole. If I tried to take a step in another direction, again a hole blocked my way. As I looked around me, I saw that the entire floor was full of holes. I wasn't fully asleep yet, but I couldn't control my imagination. I must have fallen asleep before I had time to cry out.

Our family home contained one bedroom for my parents, one room for the three smaller girls and a third room for Margaret and Ilona. Their room opened onto the yard. We also had a small dining room and a kitchen. We didn't have an indoor bathroom or toilet. The toilet was in the yard in a wooden shed. In the kitchen, we had a small tub for bathing. There were two other sheds in the yard. In one, Mother kept large quantities of flour, goose fat, jam, sugar and other groceries needed for our household. The other shed contained wood for the stoves.

The monthly wash day was a big event, as Mother changed all our bed linens. Mother hired a washerwoman, who washed the laundry all day long in a big wooden tub. I felt so sorry for the woman when I saw her hands, all wrinkled and white from the strong alkaline soap she used. But when I went to bed at night, I loved the smell of the fresh linen.

Elizabeth and I were close in age, and we played together often. We played house with our rag doll and our tiny, naked porcelain doll, which was only about eight centimetres tall. The porcelain doll's arms could move, but not its legs. I didn't have that small doll for long anyway because, being porcelain, it broke into pieces when I accidentally dropped it.

When we played, we spread our few toys on the kitchen table and kneeled on chairs so that we could reach them. We took our dolls to visit each other and put them on the furniture we had made from boxes covered with little coloured rags. I even made a doll carriage from a shoebox. At one end, I put the lid of the box upright. On the opposite end, I fastened string to allow me to pull my carriage. For the inside, I made curtains from two panels of cloth, as well as a blanket and pillow. We were so involved in our play that we spoke to our dolls as if they were real babies.

On the rare occasion that we got some sweets, I would pretend that I had finished mine but hide the last piece behind my back and say to Elizabeth, "I finished my chocolate. If you give me yours, you are an angel. If not, then you are a devil." Elizabeth would give it to me, and afterwards I would show her the piece in my hand to tease her.

We fought, as most sisters do. Our sister Aranka wasn't very happy about having us around, because she was older and often had to babysit. As the middle child, I was often left out. Elizabeth was a sickly baby from birth and needed more attention and special food. Since Aranka was older, she was always first when it came to a new winter coat or pair of shoes. But I was always on good terms with my older sister, and when we were fighting, I was always the one who apologized, no matter whose fault it was.

I remember a day when Mother was sitting on a low chair in the kitchen. The chair was either Elizabeth's or mine. It had a brown wooden back, and the seat was woven from strong, yellowish straw. She was peeling potatoes, and I saw tears pouring down her face. As a five-year-old, I was scared that something terrible had happened. Mother always seemed a little unhappy, but I had never thought much about it until this moment. "Why do you cry, Mommy? Don't cry," I said, putting my arms around her neck.

Mother wiped away her tears and said, "Go put your good dress on. All of you are going to the synagogue."

"Is today a holiday?" I asked.

"No, today is no holiday, but your big sister is going to get married," replied my mother.

"What is 'married'?" I asked.

"She will have a husband to live with, like your father and me."

I ran to get dressed, still not knowing what all the crying and fuss was about. I felt very important when I saw the crowd in front of our house waiting for the bride to appear. Then a carriage with two horses came up to our door. My sister Ilona called out, "Margaret, the carriage is here!"

Margaret came out from her room. I had never seen her look so beautiful! She wore a white dress and a headpiece decorated with flowers and lace. A white veil hung down to her ankles. She went to the carriage with Father and Ilona. Inside, there was a man whom I had never seen before. Another man, who was sitting at the front of the carriage, flicked his whip and the horses started to gallop. We, the smaller girls, did not ride with them, and I was heartbroken.

I didn't know at that time that the situation between my mother and her two stepdaughters was so bad that my eldest sister, who was twenty, married the first man who asked her. My father was a good and soft-hearted man who couldn't make peace between his wife and older daughters.

Ilona was at home a few more years after Margaret's marriage to Vilmos. Without Margaret's influence, the situation at home improved. Then Ilona got married, also when she was twenty years old, but it was a marriage of love. Her husband, Leslie, who was twenty-five, worked as a clerk for an insurance company. They moved to Baja, a fairly big city a few hours by train from Pécs. They had a son, George, in 1926. Elizabeth and I took turns visiting them and we loved to babysit our little nephew.

Unfortunately, Margaret and Mother were not on speaking terms for years. After her marriage, whenever Margaret came to the city to see our father in his shop, Mother, who was there most of the day,

walked out when she saw Margaret. Mother must have been so terribly hurt by Margaret's behaviour during the time she had lived in our
home that she still didn't wish to see her after all those years.

Despite this ill feeling between Mother and Margaret, we girls
went to visit Margaret in the little village where she lived with her
husband. The place was so small it had only one general store, which
was owned by my brother-in-law. During my visits as a little girl, I
liked to help out at the store. I learned how to make a cone-shaped
bag out of a piece of paper and pour the merchandise, such as salt, red
pepper or yeast, into it. I also liked to be there because I had the privilege of opening the big glass jars and digging into them for chocolate
bonbons and other candies.

I played with the other young girls who lived in the village, and
I liked village life, but not for very long. Later, when I grew older, I
often thought about my sister, who was a city girl, and how she had
buried herself so young in a place where she had no friends and no
entertainment. Their home consisted of only a kitchen and one other
room, both of which were spotless. There was no running water and
no indoor toilet. They had to carry buckets of water from the well in
the yard into the house. The toilet, in the back of the yard, was a deep
hole in the ground, covered by a wooden platform with a hole in the
middle and enclosed by a wooden wall with a door.

On weekends, our father often went to visit his eldest daughter,
but our mother was never invited. Not long ago, looking through my
old photographs, I found a picture of my father. He had sent it to
Margaret as a postcard in 1933, with this message written on the back:
"Father sends his picture to you, and he also wants to inform you that
he will go to see you on Saturday night. I'll also visit you on Friday
morning. We both send our love." In the photograph, Father is wearing his work clothes – a pair of worn-out pants, a flannelette shirt and
a sweater – and he is standing in front of his shop on one of the three
steps. His white hair is covered with a cap. On either side of the door
are cans, buckets and a couple of dishes for milking cows. To the left

of the door on the outside wall is a sign saying he will fix, at low cost, plumbing and old, worn-out household items.

During one of Margaret's visits to see our father in his shop, Aranka, who was then about sixteen years old, was there. When Margaret entered, my mother, as usual, got up to leave. But Aranka gently pushed Mother back onto her seat and then turned to Margaret and asked, "Don't you think it's time to ask Mother's forgiveness?" Then she said to Mother, "And you, Mother, have to accept Margaret's apology no matter what has happened in the past."

For a few minutes, Margaret just stood there. Finally, she went over to Mother and said, "Forgive me, Mother, for what I did to you, but I was just a little girl and I missed my own mother very much. I was angry with Father for having a new wife. I didn't want a new mother. I was told by everyone that stepmothers are bad. Now I know that you are not."

Before Mother could open her mouth, Margaret grabbed her hand and kissed it. This gesture pleased Mother so much that she stood up and hugged Margaret. Aranka was delighted that she was able to make peace between her sister and her mother.

The First Scars

Although my parents were not very religious, Mother kept the Jewish traditions and cooked kosher meals. Friday night, which is the beginning of the Sabbath, was my favourite time of the entire week. On Friday afternoon, we girls took turns cleaning the kitchen for the Sabbath. I would scrub the wooden floor and the black iron stove until they gleamed, then cover the table with a white linen tablecloth and put the copper candlesticks, which I had also polished, on it. Before sundown, Mother would light the candles. Aranka, Elizabeth and I would circle around her, waiting our turn to be blessed. "May the Almighty bless you, dear daughters, as he blessed our ancestors, Sarah, Rebecca, Rachel and Leah."

Because of the hard economic times after World War I, my parents didn't have many pleasures in their life. One of my father's few luxuries was smoking his pipe, which I seldom saw him without. He also lit a cigar once a week. On his birthday or other special occasions, we always gave him a few good cigars as a present, and he saved them for Sundays. Also, on Sunday afternoons, as his special treat, he would go to the city's coffee house for his afternoon card game. Elizabeth and I used to visit him there, hoping that he was winning, because then he would give us some money to buy candies or chocolate. But if he was losing the game, he would angrily send us home.

Sometimes Mother begged him not to go to the coffee house and to take the family for a picnic instead. We had a favourite place for these outings, a park on a hill called Tettye. The word comes from the Turkish word *tekke*, monastery, and one had been built there many centuries ago, when Hungary was under Turkish occupation. Some ruins of the monastery still remained, making it a wonderful playground for hide-and-seek.

We girls loved to go on those infrequent outings. They were the only time when our parents paid attention to us. Any other time, they were busy with their daily routines and work. For our outings, Mother would pack sandwiches and buy soft drinks in little bottles from vendors. Those drinks were red and sweet. There was also a vendor selling salty pretzels, which he carried on a long stick held upright. We would nag our mother until she gave in and bought a pretzel for each of us. We spent lovely afternoons in that park. My parents usually found some people to talk to, and my sisters and I would play with their children.

~

On the first Monday of every month, my parents went to a market to sell enamel pots and pans as well as goods from our store. In the tinsmith shop they owned, Father made buckets, cake pans and other metal household items.

When I was about seven or eight years old, I was allowed to go to the market with my parents. They rented a huge carriage with two strong horses to carry all the goods, which were carefully wrapped in straw. The market was an interesting place, and I liked to wander around. Although there were some tents, almost everything was laid on the open ground or on long tables.

First, I had to help my parents unpack and carry the wares to the square that was appointed for their display. Merchandise was grouped together in the market. All textiles were in one row, porcelain and glass were in another, fresh food from the farms – dairy products, vegetables, fruits – in other groups. I can still taste the freshly made butter, which was sold on big green leaves by the peasant women.

There were tents where gingerbread was sold in shapes of animals and dolls of all sizes. But I liked the gingerbread hearts the best. They were beautifully decorated with colourful flowers made from sugar. On the brown gingerbread hearts, the pink, blue, yellow or red flowers were gorgeous, and each had a small mirror in the centre of the heart. There were even some with inscriptions on them, such as "My heart is yours forever" or "I give my heart to my sweetheart." I remember the time my mother bought me a small heart. I kept it for a while, but it was so tempting that eventually I ate it.

My favourite part of the market was the toy section. I loved to look at the dolls, cradles, doll carriages and dollhouses. "Don't touch it!" a lady screamed at me when I tried to pet a doll's tiny hand. I jerked my hand back and just looked at the beauty. Her face was rosy porcelain, and her big blue eyes with dark lashes opened and closed. She wore a pink silk dress, white socks and black patent-leather shoes. She had a white pearl necklace around her neck and a pink bow in her curly blond hair. I looked at the other dolls but went back to my favourite, whom I called Piri. How I wished that Piri would be mine to hold, rock, put in bed beside me at night and hug. I went back to tell Mother about the precious doll.

As I started to say, "Mommy, I saw the most beautiful doll in the..." my mother stopped me. "You know that I don't have money for a doll or any other toys," she said. I knew that. All I wanted was to talk to her, to tell her how nice Piri was. I had only a rag doll, which my sister Aranka had made for Elizabeth and me. The doll was filled with sawdust, which had started to come out from some parts of the doll's arms already. My heart ached.

I climbed up into the carriage and started to sweep the straw with my bare feet. Mother noticed and cried out, "Don't do that! A splinter will go into your sole." But in my anger and hurt, I just continued, until it really happened. A sharp piece of wood went deep into my flesh. I was afraid to tell my mother because she had warned me earlier.

My leg hurt for the rest of the afternoon, and I was very quiet. A few days later, our next-door neighbour noticed my leg and shrieked at my mother, "What happened to her? Her leg is all swollen up!" Only then did my mother take a closer look at my leg, which was swollen from ankle to knee. I was scared when I saw adults so concerned about me. In answer to my mother's questions, I told her about the accident on market day.

"Go wash your feet. We are going to see Dr. Szánto," said Mother.

"Do we take the streetcar, Mother?" I asked. When she said yes, I was happy, because going on a streetcar was such a treat.

After the doctor examined my foot, he asked me if I was a brave girl.

"Yes," I said, but I shivered with fright when I saw the instruments the doctor took out.

He didn't have an assistant, so he called his own mother from the other room to hold my leg. I closed my eyes tightly in anticipation of the pain. But it wasn't so bad, and after the doctor finished and bandaged my foot, he gave me a couple of candies for my bravery. I was glad it was over, because that meant another ride on the streetcar.

~

I don't remember my father's parents; I think they passed away when I was very young. I do remember my maternal grandmother, whom I saw only once. She lived in another town with her unmarried daughter, Hermina. I must have been only six years old when Mother pressed me to write a letter to Grandma. Because I had heard Mother say so many times, "My hands are shaking," I started my letter, "Dear Grandma, forgive me for my ugly writing but my hands are shaking."

Mother had two sisters whom I knew. One was Auntie Cili, who lived in Budapest, our capital city, with her two grown daughters. The other sister, Matilda, lived in a smaller city, Ozora. One year, Mother took me to visit Auntie Cili. My mother and I travelled six hours by train from Pécs to Budapest. After we got off the train, we had a short distance to walk to Auntie Cili's apartment. We passed a big amusement park on our way.

"Mother, look!" I pulled her by the hand to a merry-go-round. "Look! Those big horses and deer and those carriages! How fast they are going around!"

"Would you like to have a ride?" she asked.

"Yes! Yes! I would!" We waited until the merry-go-round stopped, and I chose a carriage and sat down. Another little girl climbed into it and took the seat across from me. That carriage was such a beautiful creation. The seats were made of red velvet with two huge angels on either side, their hands spread out above our heads as if they were protecting us from something bad. Then the merry-go-round started to go slowly around in circles.

"Hi, Mother!" I waved to her. But the merry-go-round went faster by the second, and soon I couldn't see Mother any more. I kept my eyes tightly shut and held onto the bar with both hands. I wished the ride would stop. Finally, the merry-go-round started to slow down and then stopped. Mother waved to me to catch my attention, and when I saw her, I ran to her, almost crying. She hugged and comforted me, seeing how scared I had been to not see her.

We continued our walk to my auntie's home. She and her family lived in a very large apartment house, a kind of building I had never seen in our city. My two cousins were older than me, and they kissed me and asked my name. Then they helped me to take my poor garments from the suitcase and put them into a drawer.

My auntie asked my mother, "Where are her good shoes?"

My mother pointed to the sandals I was wearing. "Those are a pair of new sandals. I just bought them last week," she said.

"I'm not taking her without black patent-leather shoes," declared my auntie. So, to my delight, I got another pair of new shoes. Usually, I got new ones only when my toes were already showing through.

Later Auntie Cili sewed me a green silk dress from one of her daughters' old dresses. I felt so elegant in my new dress and shoes.

One night, my cousins took me to a movie. It would have been my very first, but unfortunately no young children were allowed to go in. "You just stay out in the lobby until we get out. And don't you dare wander away!" my cousin told me. I still remember how bored and frightened I was to have to sit in one place for two whole hours. I felt very much alone.

On another occasion, Mother took me to Auntie Matilda's in Ozora, which was also quite far from our city. When Mother left me there, I was miserable. Auntie was very strict about eating. I had to eat everything, like it or not, and some of her cooking was very spicy.

She had a tailor shop in her home, and after her husband's death, she ran the shop with four or five assistants. One day between meals, Auntie made a salad of sliced cucumber, with sour cream on top. It tasted awful. I made a grimace that one of the helpers saw, and he suggested that I dig a hole in the garden and bury the salad. I did as I was told and took the empty bowl back to Auntie. However, it was too soon. "You already finished it? You must like it very much," said my auntie. Bam! Another portion went into the bowl.

Once, I complained to my auntie's housemaid that I didn't like my auntie. She told on me, and the next day Auntie packed my things and, without notifying my parents, put me on a train headed back home. I was only eight years old.

It was a Sunday afternoon when I arrived, and nobody was home. I climbed through the window of our house and went to bed. When the family returned, Mother almost had a heart attack when I sat up in my bed and said, "I am home, Mother."

～

I wasn't quite six years old when Mother enrolled me in a Jewish school, which I attended for my first four years of education. From almost the first day of school, my classmates mocked me. While we always had food on the table, my parents could not afford proper clothes for us. I was a pretty, petite child with huge brown eyes and black hair; however, I wasn't dressed like the other children. They noticed that I wore a summer dress as a slip under my school dress during the winter. Mother had made my scarf from a terry cloth towel with a flower printed on it. I also proudly wore a cap that Mother had made from a brown cotton stocking. She had cut off the upper part, sewed it together at one end and put a pom-pom on it. My classmates, however, made fun of the cap.

Once or twice a year, the children who were well off brought in some used clothing, and the teacher gave it away to the less fortunate ones. My teacher, noticing how poorly I was dressed, offered some of the clothing to me, but Mother wouldn't let me accept anything. That proud attitude accompanied me through those first four years.

Most of the girls in the class were rich and spoiled. One day, a girl named Edith approached me and asked, "Would you like to be my servant?" I wasn't quite sure what the word "servant" meant.

"What do I have to do as a servant?" I asked her.

"Not much," replied Edith. "You have to bring my coat from the rack, help me put it on, carry my schoolbag and all those things that a servant has to do. I will give you a pencil, a pen or an eraser, maybe even some money."

"No, I don't want to be your servant!" I replied.

"As you wish," Edith said, shrugging her shoulders. "I will find somebody else who will happily do it for me." Thinking of the things I might get from her, I reconsidered and accepted her offer.

I finished Jewish elementary school in 1926 and was then enrolled in the state-run public school. I wasn't the best student there, but I did well in subjects that I liked, such as German, or those taught by a teacher I liked, such as science, which was taught by Miss Ilonka. In this school, I made some friends and thankfully did not have to put up with the mocking and humiliation that I had endured in elementary school. But those times had left scars.

After I completed schooling in the state-run public school, Mother asked me what I wanted to do. I could go to business school for a couple of years and become a secretary, as my sister Aranka had done, or I could begin an apprenticeship in a dressmaker's shop. I chose the latter.

For one and a half years, I learned the dressmaking trade. For the first six months, I did everything but sew. I had to babysit, dust furniture and do other household chores. Then, I learned to sew. I graduated, but I never became a dressmaker. I never much liked dressmaking, and I didn't have the talent to be a good seamstress. Or maybe I remembered when the boss's domestic help had told me, "Ibi, you will never become a dressmaker." Nonetheless, I worked for a few more years and earned a small salary.

Zolti

I was fifteen years old when I joined a Zionist organization. I was very active in the group and even wrote small articles in its monthly paper. We talked about many topics, read Darwin and Freud, and learned the Hebrew language. We were preparing for living in a kibbutz in Israel, which was then called British Mandate Palestine.

I enjoyed being in that group. We went for excursions in our wonderful mountains and I marvelled at the huge pine trees, colourful wildflowers, prattling little streams and different birdsongs. I could listen for hours to birds as they answered one another's calls.

My best memories were of our group's camping trip. It took a while to convince my parents to let me go. The campsite was near the border of Czechoslovakia, in the Mátra Mountains, which were famous for their beauty and natural hot springs. Almost every night, we built a campfire and entertained ourselves by reading poems, performing short plays or singing beautiful Hebrew songs. We slept in tents on straw mattresses. The boys' tents were separated from those of the girls. Our counsellors were responsible young adults. But the boys still pulled pranks on the girls. One night, two of the boys came into our tent. Since they believed that I was sleeping, they pulled my mattress outside, with me on it. I pretended not to wake up, so as not to spoil their fun. Another night, the boys painted some of the girls' faces – fortunately not mine – with black shoe polish.

Our three weeks of camping came to an end all too soon and we were saying our farewells, sitting together around the fire, sipping our tea, eating cookies, talking and singing. A boy who had arrived at the campfire a little later than me sat down beside me. I had seen him many times before and was attracted to him, but he was constantly surrounded by girls and he didn't even know I existed, or so I thought. He was very handsome, tall and slim with wavy brown hair and brown eyes. His nose was a bit prominent in his narrow face, but I liked that, too. I felt lucky that he had sat beside me.

He introduced himself as Zoltán Rechnitzer, Zolti for short, and asked my name. He came from the city of Pápa and was eighteen years old. We talked about our cities, books we had read, movies we had seen and other subjects. Before the end of the night, we exchanged addresses. We corresponded for years.

I had a few girlfriends from school – Lily Neuman, Piri Schlanger and Gizi Stern – who had also joined the Zionist movement. I still treasure a photo from that time that shows me with my girlfriends in uniform. We wore navy blue skirts, grey cotton blouses and royal-blue triangle neckties. Gizi, my best friend, also had a boyfriend from another city, and they too corresponded with each other.

Gizi and I spent many evenings together in our homes. We made the night romantic by shutting the lights and opening the ceramic stove's outer door so that we could see only the glow from the burning wood in the dark. We talked about our wishes and dreams and about boys, and we read the letters from our boyfriends to each other.

Occasionally I met other boys from the group. One hot summer day, one of these boys, a medical student named Sándor, escorted me home. Mother called him in and asked, "Would you like some cold watermelon?" "Yes, Aunt Szalai. Thank you," he answered. He won my mother's heart immediately with these simple words, spoken without any reluctance. Mother was disappointed that I didn't like Sándor because of the pimples on his face.

During the almost two years I corresponded with Zolti, we came to know and love each other through long monthly letters. In our letters, we recorded everything that had happened in our young lives. If I saw a good movie, I described its content. I also wrote about books I had read, and often we exchanged our opinions or even argued about these books in our letters. Zolti often wrote that I was intelligent and pretty and that he was in love with me. His letters built up my self-confidence, previously lacking. We fell deeper and deeper in love. He was my whole world.

He visited me a few times, and my parents liked him, too. Zolti was an only child. His parents were poor, and they wanted a wealthy girl for their son, so they opposed our friendship. When Zolti's letters started to come more infrequently and finally stopped, I was devastated. I became more and more withdrawn by the day. I lost interest in everything. Mother took me to a doctor, and he said that I was under tremendous stress and advised me to go to a hospital for some medication and rest.

In the hospital, I wanted to be left alone and didn't want to see anybody from my family, not even my mother. I loved my parents, but they were busy making a living and didn't have time for me. I had not heard a word from Zolti, and I was very hurt. I was eighteen years old, and he had been my first and only love since I was fifteen. I was sure that his parents had forbidden him to see me or write to me. I tried not to think of my sweetheart anymore.

A short time later, I felt better and was discharged from the hospital. The doctor then suggested that a change in my environment would be most helpful. Mother wrote to my sister Aranka asking her to take me in for a while and find a job for me. By this time, Aranka had already been married for a couple of years and lived in Budapest with her husband, Jenö.

Aranka and Jenö took me in, and Jenö got a job for me in a thread factory, where I worked ten hours a day. At first, my life was very simple. After work, having stood on my feet for those long hours, I went home dead tired. After supper, I washed myself and went to bed. Early the next morning, I started my daily routine again. This continued for some time. I was quiet and withdrawn for a while, but gradually I started to talk with my colleagues and to read books on weekends. I had always enjoyed reading, and sitting on the corner of the couch with a good book became my favourite pastime again. I especially remember reading Margaret Mitchell's *Gone with the Wind*, in Hungarian translation.

One day, I opened a drawer in my sister's kitchen and found an open envelope with a letter inside addressed to me. It was in Zolti's handwriting. My sister had hidden it from me; maybe she had meant well, but she didn't know how I had waited every day for a word, a message, a hint from him. I wanted to forget him, but I couldn't. And here was a letter from him that hadn't been given to me! With shaking hands, I took the letter out of the envelope and started to read. I had to stop a few times to wipe away my tears.

Zolti wrote that he had gotten my address from my parents and that he still loved me. He had heard I was sick and felt responsible for it. He would be coming to Budapest soon, and he wanted to see me. I was in seventh heaven after reading these words!

Five or six weeks later, I moved out of my sister's place and rented a bed from a single elderly lady who also provided meals for a reasonable price. But I didn't stay there very long either. I had made friends with a girl who was also alone and only a couple of years older than me, and we decided to move in together. This move was good for both of us. We shared our expenses, and we also became good companions. My new friend, Babus, was a little on the chubby side and a bit taller than me. She had big, beautiful blue eyes. Her hair was naturally curly and blond, in contrast to mine.

One summer day, Babus had a date, and I was alone at home in the little garden behind the house, in a lounge chair reading a book. My hair was in rollers, drying under the sun. Suddenly, I had the feeling that somebody was watching me. I looked up, and there was Zolti looking down at me! There are no words to describe the surprise and joy I felt at that moment. He helped me up from the chair and hugged me. We clung to each other, tears streaming down our faces. He was not ashamed to show his feelings.

"You love me! You still love me!" I repeated over and over.

Even now, tears well up in my eyes as I write about that meeting. I love him with every beat of my heart. I always did and I always will. When I thought that I had lost him and tried to accept it, he came back. "We belong together, darling," he said. "I'll never leave you again."

Zolti told me that he had had a fight with his parents over me. He had left his hometown of Pápa and was now working in Budapest, renting a room with another young man. During the summer, we dated as much as we could. Our salaries were only enough for everyday living, and very seldom could we afford such luxuries as a movie, a beer or an espresso, which he liked. We went to the beach or museums or window-shopped, all free activities. Occasionally we went to a restaurant to eat an inexpensive meal. We took long walks hand in hand, and we were happy. Very happy.

In 1938, Zolti's parents moved from Pápa to Budapest. Zolti had made amends with his parents, but as far as I knew he didn't speak to them about me. However, one day he announced, "Dress up nicely, darling. We are going to see my parents. I want them to know you."

I was very excited. "What will I tell them? Will they like me? How do I look?" I showered him with questions.

"Just be yourself. You are okay. You are pretty," Zolti said.

I was very nervous when we arrived at his parents' home at 16 Népszinház utca. His mother was kind and friendly to me. I resembled her a little bit. She was short like me, with dark hair and brown eyes. Her face was round, and her long hair was in two braids wrapped around the crown of her head. She was a simple and good-hearted person with not much education but with a natural brightness. She dressed very simply and absolutely refused to wear a hat.

Zolti's father was handsome and tall, like his son, but he had blue eyes and light-coloured hair. He wore eyeglasses. His nose was slightly turned up, which made him look more gentile than Jewish. He dressed elegantly and looked very distinguished. He was educated and intelligent.

I had the feeling that Zolti's parents were not a perfect match, but they had a good marriage. They welcomed me into the family. Zolti's father said that although I didn't have any dowry and was not rich, I did have a job and was a diligent worker.

Both of Zolti's parents agreed to our marriage, and we planned for a wedding in the near future. But first we wanted to visit my parents in Pécs. In those years, there was a "penny express" that, for less than half the price of regular train fare, would take people from Budapest to some of Hungary's other cities for a day. We bought two tickets, and on an early Sunday morning we met in the west railway station. Zolti surprised me by wearing a new grey-striped suit, which he had bought for this occasion. He was so handsome, and I was so proud of him.

My parents were terribly happy for me, and they took Zolti into their hearts. We had only one day in Pécs, but I even had some time to introduce my fiancé to my girlfriends. My younger sister, Elizabeth, who had very recently married and lived with her in-laws, came home with her new husband to be with us on this special day.

Mother prepared a lovely lunch, which we ate outdoors in the little courtyard among the colourful and fragrant flowers. Oh, how happy I was among my loved ones! Yet, involuntarily, I thought back to the time not long before when I had been so miserable and believed there was no end to it in sight. I had never thought I would be this happy. That day ended too soon, and at night everybody escorted us to the railway station to say goodbye.

When Zolti had saved enough money, he bought an engagement ring for me, which was also a wedding band. It was not traditional to buy separate rings for engagements and weddings. Instead, during the engagement, the bride-to-be wore the ring on the ring finger of her left hand and after the wedding moved the ring to the right hand. While we were showing the ring to Zolti's mother, it fell to the floor and rolled away. "Bad luck," my mother-in-law said.

We were engaged for about a year before getting married in the fall of 1939, when Europe was on the threshold of war. My parents went into debt to give us money for a bedroom set, because they had given one to each of their other four daughters when they got married. My father came to the wedding at the Nagyfuvaros synagogue, but Mother was so sick she couldn't come. It was a very simple wedding: Zolti had to borrow an overcoat from a friend, and we didn't even have enough money for a wedding dress. I wore a navy-blue pleated skirt, a white blouse, a three-quarter-length navy-blue coat, a little white hat with a veil and a pair of navy-blue shoes. Father was very proud when he overheard somebody say, "The bride is very pretty."

My in-laws gave us just enough money to go to a nice restaurant and to a hotel for our wedding night. Mama and Papa, as I called my in-laws, were good to us. We couldn't afford our own place, so we shared their two-bedroom apartment, which had only two rooms plus a kitchen and a toilet. We didn't even have a bathroom. Since one of the rooms was rented to a young couple, we put a bed in the kitchen. This served as our bedroom until the tenants moved out. My mother-in-law did the cooking during the whole time we lived together.

I had a steady job in the thread factory, where I worked in shifts either from six in the morning until two in the afternoon or from two in the afternoon until ten at night. Some days, Zolti and I could meet only late at night. On those days, I left little notes for Zolti with messages, such as, "Be careful. I just washed the floor." Zolti would answer on the note, "I was careful."

Zolti was a mechanic for various items, such as sewing machines and radios. He also mastered podiatry and massage. He preferred to work at the latter and often worked in spas, of which there were many in Budapest. My father-in-law also worked in thermal spas, and he was well known as a podiatrist because of his good work with his patients. Later, when he was not allowed to work in the spas due to the anti-Jewish laws, my father-in-law worked at home. He made two curtained-off compartments, and had many patients.

After about six months, Zolti and I moved into the inner room. We bought a combination of bedroom and living room furniture from the money that Father had given us. There was a divan, which we opened at night for sleeping, a small round table and two arm-chairs, an end table with a lamp and a wardrobe. I made white curtains and gold tablecloths from lace. Every little piece we made or bought was a treasure for us, and our room was cozy.

Our entertainment consisted of playing Monopoly with our friends, seeing a movie or, seldom, a play at the theatre. Zolti's favourite actor was Fred Astaire, and we saw every one of his films. In the summertime, we went to beaches, strolled along the banks of the Danube River or window-shopped in the elegant boutiques. To buy some necessity such as a pair of shoes or a dress or suit was an event. Once, I lost a pair of leather gloves, and I was upset for days.

Zolti had a simple little camera, and he took nice photographs, but he wished to have a better camera, so he saved his pennies and finally had enough. We went from shop to shop until he got what he wanted for a reasonable price. After we got out of the store, he grabbed me and kissed me all over my face.

"What was all this kissing for?" I asked him.

"Because you let me buy it," he said with happiness.

~

It was a cold winter day in 1941 when Zolti and I went to a doctor because I suspected that I was pregnant. Because of the war, we hadn't planned to have any children. When the doctor confirmed that I was three months pregnant, I left the office crying and went right into my husband's open arms. I was frightened and confused when I told him the news. Those were uncertain times, and I wondered what the future would hold for a Jewish child.

Zolti said, "Don't cry, darling. We need this baby. You will see." My dearest didn't know how true those words would prove to be. Later, when I calmed down, like most mothers-to-be, I had many questions. Would the baby be a boy or a girl? Whom would it resemble?

My in-laws were happy, and when I confided my doubts to Mama, she said, "If God gave a lamb, he will certainly give pasture ground." I started to sew baby things, and Zolti made a shelf for the baby's clothes. From time to time, I took out the baby clothes and imagined my child in them. I was healthy and strong and worked almost to the end of my pregnancy.

By the time my child's birthdate arrived, the hatred for Jews was worsening across Europe. It was a hot summer night on July 16, 1942, when I was awakened by labour pains. When I turned on the light on the end table, I saw that the clock showed 4:00 a.m. Since I didn't want to wake Zolti, I waited a couple of hours and the pains stopped. My husband went to work because I insisted, but later in the morning the pains started again. I told Mama they were coming every ten minutes or so. She calmly took out the wooden tub we used for washing clothes and bathing. She gave me a bath and helped me to get dressed.

The clinic where I had gone for monthly check-ups and lectures about baby care was walking distance away. Mama escorted me there, but, to my surprise, the hospital staff said there was no bed for me. It was suggested that I could either lie on the floor or go somewhere else. Since this was the clinic that I had visited during my pregnancy and my pains were getting stronger, I agreed to stay on the floor. Fortunately, I got a bed after all. It seemed that the clinic's intention had been to make things difficult for me because I was a Jew.

At about 2:00 p.m., my pains were so strong that they took me into the delivery room. When Zolti telephoned, he was told not to come because they didn't expect the baby to be born until the next day. I watched the clock, so that is how I know that my son was born a few minutes after 5:00 p.m. on the same day. I had been too excited to eat anything the whole day, so I was very hungry after the delivery. It took a long time before I was given a glass of milk. I was wheeled to a corridor and left there for hours. Only after many hours did I receive the required attention. I hoped that they were providing my baby with better care.

The next day, my husband and his parents came to visit. Zolti lovingly held the baby's tiny fingers and said how beautiful and perfect our son was. He already talked about how we would raise our son to be an athlete like his daddy.

The atmosphere in the hospital was terrible. War was everywhere in Europe. Although the Nazis had not yet entered Hungary, hatred of Jews was already evident. Each baby lay in a little basket at the foot of his or her mother's bed. One day, a mother screamed for a doctor when she saw that her infant had vomited blood. When the doctor came running, the nurse in charge said to him, "Don't run, doctor. It is only a Jewish bastard." I was happy that I could leave the hospital with our son, András, within five days.

Zolti bought a second-hand baby carriage. He cleaned and polished it, and it looked like new. We were happy and proud of our little son. It was so good to hold him in my arms. I wished that I could protect him from every bad thing that might come. Unfortunately, I could not protect him for very long.

Andy was four months old when his father was taken away to a labour battalion. The Hungarian government had been drafting Jewish men into a segregated section of the army, where they were forced to do miserable work and were treated terribly. Zolti was allowed visiting days only once every couple of months to see us. He was so caring and protective of our child during those short times.

Andy was seven or eight months old when, as I held him in my arms, he hit my face. Of course, as a baby, he didn't know what he was doing. But Zolti, who was home on leave, gently took the baby's hand and said, "Never, ever hit your mother."

My in-laws adored the child, and they wanted me to stay home to take care of him. Our apartment felt unhealthy because it had no natural light; it was dark and damp. I made it a point to take Andy to the nearby park every day and spent many hours there with him.

In late spring of 1943, when Andy was ten months old, I decided to take him to see my parents in Pécs. They had sold the family house and rented a one-bedroom apartment near their shop. Andy was their third grandchild. The first had been Ilona's son, George, born in 1926. Aranka's daughter, Marianna, who was seven years older than Andy, was the second. Neither Margaret nor Elizabeth had children.

My parents were so pleased to see us and meet the new baby. Mother was happiest when she took Andy for walks in his stroller. She babysat when my father and I went to a movie. Father had built a small crib for the child. My parents had an easier life now that all their daughters were out of the house.

Early one morning, when my visit with them was almost over, there was a knock on the door and, to our surprise, Zolti walked in. He stayed a day or two, and then we went home together. My husband had been sent home from the forced labour service and told he could stay for a while. Andy could already say "Daddy Zolti" in his special baby talk.

The Letter

Somehow, we hadn't paid much attention to what had been happening for years to Jews everywhere in Europe. We were young and optimistic, hoping that the terrible things would not affect us. Then they did. On March 19, 1944, the Germans invaded Hungary. After that, life got progressively worse every day.

Restrictive laws for Jews came into force. We were not allowed to go to any public places, such as cinemas or restaurants. We had to surrender our radios to the government. Only at certain times of the day could we go out to buy food or to the park. On the streetcars, we could sit only at the back.

Starting on April 6, every Jew age six and older had to wear a yellow star on his or her chest. The next month, all men aged eighteen to sixty were called into the forced labour service. Zolti was taken away. Buildings in some districts in Budapest were designated as "Jewish houses" and huge yellow stars were affixed to their fronts. Our building became one. We were allowed to stay in our home, but we had to take in other Jewish people. My husband's two female cousins moved in with us.

There was a nice little pastry shop on our street, and the friendly owner adored my son. As I was not allowed to go in, I used to write notes and give them to Andy, who was then a toddler, along with some money, saying, "Be careful, sweetheart. Hold the money tight, give it to the lady and she will give you your favourite torte. You are a big boy, and I am going to let you go in alone and wait for you outside." Andy would get his pastry, and the owner escorted him back to me with a kiss on his cheek.

One time, we were riding on a streetcar, and because our time to be out on the street was over, I wasn't wearing the yellow star. Suddenly in the quiet vehicle, my son asked, "Mommy, where is your yellow star?" Fortunately, only I could understand my lisping son's question. Pointing out the window, I quickly said, "Look at those big trucks with many soldiers on them!" Andy was satisfied and didn't demand an answer. If any of our fellow Hungarians on the streetcar had understood my child's question, we would have suffered dire consequences.

My sister Aranka's bungalow in Zugló, on the outskirts of the city, was also designated as a "Jewish house." She took in our sister Elizabeth and some friends of their family. After October 1944, our communication abruptly ceased, and I didn't know what happened to them until after our liberation.

By the end of November, a ghetto was formed in the heart of the city. What happened from that point on is described in a letter I wrote on January 30, 1945, only two weeks after our liberation from the ghetto. The purpose of my letter was to write down what had happened to us, while it was fresh in my memory, and give it to Zolti, who I was sure would come out of that hell alive. I still have the original letter, written in pencil by the light of a single candle, the pages now yellowed with time and the words faded away.

Budapest, January 30, 1945
My dearest love!
Nine months ago, on May 9, 1944, when you kissed me goodbye, I told you my life would be worthless if you did not come back. "I will be back, sweetheart, because I love you and our little son. Don't worry, my dear," you replied to me. Now we are home and safe and so are your

parents, and I feel that you will come home, too. I feel it very strongly. Our little son prays for you every night with his tiny hands clasped together.

Where should I begin to tell you of our sufferings? I want to tell you everything that has happened to us. Maybe I'll go back to October 15, 1944. Our Regent, Horthy, spoke on the radio, and we were told that Hungary would no longer fight in the war, so nobody had to worry. We were tremendously glad to hear it. We had all crowded into the yard of our building to hear our Regent's declaration from the janitor's radio. We were jumping with joy and tearing off the yellow stars from our chests. We thought it was the end of our sufferings. We had had enough. The yellow stars were discriminatory – unlike other citizens, we were not allowed to go out of the house except between five and seven in the evening to buy groceries, and of course by that time there were not many groceries left. We were forbidden to go to any public places like cafeterias, soda shops, movies or playgrounds. On the streetcars or buses we could only sit at the back. In many of the stores you could read this: "Dogs and Jews forbidden to enter." There were many other awful things but now we thought that an end had finally come to these orders. We were wrong. Even more bad things started. Our Regent had the best intentions, but he was weak, and on the same day, the fascist Arrow Cross Party, with its leader, Ferenc Szálasi, took over the presidency. Szálasi was bloodthirsty. He swore that he would help the Germans to annihilate the Jews.

The next morning I saw sixty or more people – men, women and children – marching with their hands raised above their heads. Fascists escorted them. Later on the same day, some police and fascists with swastikas on their arms came to our building. One of them roared, "Every Jew down to the yard or I shoot!" We were very scared. You know, dear, by then about three hundred people lived in the building, most of them Jews. We had no time to pack anything. I just grabbed the knapsack, little Andy's winter coat and a blanket. Those things were all ready in case of an air raid. We had to raise our hands like criminals and form a double line in front of the house. When Andy heard those words "hands up" he took his hand out of mine and raised his, too.

First they took us to the nearest open ground and robbed us. We had to throw all money, wristwatches, rings and flashlights on a blanket. We had to put our hands up again so they could inspect if any rings were left. If they found something, they beat our hands with a whip. I put my wedding band in Andy's coat pocket. I wanted to save it.

After we were robbed, we were ordered to form a double line once more and to march to an unknown place. While we were marching, still with raised hands, you couldn't imagine what the crowd on the sidewalks did to us. They were enjoying watching our march. They hit us and spat on us. One man grabbed the blanket from my hand, so Andy had no cover for the night. Others took the coats off of people's shoulders. One man beat your father and smashed his eyeglasses. At that point, Andy and I lost your parents in the crowd. On the route, I saw that we were being led to the Tattersall racetrack. There, we spent two horrible days and nights. It was like a nightmare. When we arrived, it was already dark. We had to sit down on the bare ground, which was covered with dung from the horses. There were a lot of people, collected from every part of the city. Many of them didn't even have a place to sit, so they stood all night. The children fell asleep in their mother's laps. Andy too fell asleep and I hugged him all night to keep him warm. We adults were awake the whole night waiting for the morning. What would happen to us? Finally, morning came. We were ordered once more to form a line of four and to walk around a platform where some Arrow Cross bandits were pointing machine guns at us. One of them roared, "You rotten Jews! All of you will die within a few hours." But nothing had happened yet except that we had no food, water or roof above our heads.

During the day we walked all over the place looking for Mama and Papa. There were Arrow Cross women with whips, and they hit everybody around them. I tried to avoid those beasts. From time to time, Andy and I sat down on the ground and I fed him some crackers and apples from the knapsack. I couldn't take a bite. After that, we again went to look for your parents. Finally in mid-afternoon, we found each other. We were crying and hugging to try to comfort each other. We all sat down on the ground again to try to keep Andy warm. Then came the second night. About 3 a.m. we suddenly saw a bright light and a man on a loudspeaker announced that we could all go home. The order came from the chief, Szálasi, who had become the head of the government. As soon as we got out, German soldiers shot among us at random. Many were wounded and killed, but somehow we got home. Little Andy's first words were "Hello, my red tricycle. You say hello to me, too." You know, dear, he had just received that red tricycle from Joe, our superintendent, before we were taken away.

After we got home, no Jews were allowed to go out on the streets for three days. Arrow Cross Party members searched us to prepare to take us to labour camps. All women of up to fifty years of age and all men up to sixty were to go. Your father was taken away. I worried every minute of the day. I decided not to go but to hide somewhere. During the night I slept fully clothed, on top of the bed in case they came for me during the night. I had decided to hide in a closet or under the bed.

One morning, soldiers and policemen came to our building with a written order that every woman between the ages of eighteen and fifty had to leave for the labour camps. We could take some food and clothes with us. We had just gotten ready to go to the appointed place when another order came with another soldier. He said that those women whose husbands or fathers were already in a labour battalion could stay home.

But not for long. Two days later, another order came saying that every woman had to go, no matter where her husband or father was. I didn't want to go, but I couldn't hide either because I had no other documents but my own, which said I was a Jew. Some women had false papers and were able to hide.

Before I was ready to go, I heard good news. On Columbus utca, there was a Red Cross home and children could go there to stay. The next night it was raining, and about twenty-five children went to that place. The janitor arranged for two nice policemen to escort us to prevent the crowds from lynching us. On the way, I told Andy, "Darling, you will see what a nice place we are going to. There will be many little white beds for babies, lots of toys and nice nurses who will take care of you." I really meant what I told him. How could I have been so naïve? The poor child was so happy to hear it that I had to tell him over and over.

The whole time we were walking, the rain poured down. There was darkness; no lights were allowed because of the air raids. Dead people were still lying in front of the buildings on the sidewalk. We almost stepped on them. That afternoon there had been a terrible air raid and heavy bombing that had damaged houses and killed many. Those attacks came every day and nobody knew who would be next to die.

By the time we arrived, we were soaking wet. At last we entered the Red Cross house. However, there were no little beds, nurses, food or lights. In the darkness we moved to the cellar, which was already crowded. I put my overcoat on the floor in a corner, took off Andy's wet shoes and coat and laid him on the floor. He fell asleep immediately. Somehow we arranged a little place for all the children to lie down.

Darling, can you imagine that in this building, which was big enough for about six hundred people, there were already three thousand? And still people came. People, young and old, who had escaped from labour camps, children without parents, babies with their mothers. There were orphans and crippled children, all of them very dirty and sick, with lice in their hair. Children who had been well cared for, clean and beautiful, at home with their parents. But their parents had been killed or taken away to labour or concentration camps, and neighbours had to put the children in that home and leave them there. I was lucky to be with Andy. We were there a little over two weeks. It is so hard to tell you how terrible those two weeks were. After that, Andy got sick and I went home with him to Mama.

One Saturday afternoon, we were sleeping when Mama came into the room to wake me. Her face was pale and her hands were shaking. "Ibi, my child, you have to escape with the baby again. The policemen and Arrow Cross members are going door to door. They want to collect us. I don't know where they will take us. You and Andy have to escape."

I took out a suitcase and put some clothes in it, among them your nice new pyjamas and shirt, which I bought for you and which you liked very much. I told Mama to come with us. It took some time to convince her. Finally she agreed and we went back to the Red Cross home. A few hours later they took away all the remaining Jews from the building. The younger ones were taken to the railway station where they would be sent to camps, the older people were taken to the ghetto. I thought that no matter how awful the Red Cross home was, at least we would be safe. Safe, but for how long?

Not very long. The authorities had noticed that people were hiding there. I was sure our fellow Hungarians had denounced us. On December 3, 1944, policemen and Arrow Cross bandits who called themselves soldiers encircled the building. Once more we had to go to the yard. I saw some women lying on the ground. When I saw the white foam around their mouths, I looked in the other direction – they had committed suicide. Unable to bear the ordeal any longer, they had taken poison they had kept for this final use. I couldn't stand the sight of them. You should have waited for this final act, I thought. Maybe there is still hope for life.

The same thing happened again. We were robbed of everything that had any value. This time, I had hidden my wedding band and some money in Andy's diaper. All of us were ordered to go to a stadium, where we were sorted into two groups – one for the young people, another for the older ones and young mothers with babies under one year. Andy was two years and two months old. Those little ones who were over one had to be left behind, or strangers could take them to the ghetto.

My dear God! How terrible it was to hear the children crying for their mothers, and mothers screaming for their children. The people who did this to us had no hearts at all, only stones in their chests.

Mama and I were always at the end of the line. You remember what your mother used to say? "Those who gain time can save their lives." I put a black kerchief on my head in an attempt to hide my face. I *couldn't. A policeman came over and roared, "Can't you hear? Are you deaf? Young ones over there!"*

I put Andy in Mama's arms. He was screaming, "Mommy! Mommy! Don't go, don't leave me!" My heart wanted to fall apart. I told Mama to come after me. It was a good idea because she saw a policeman she knew from her hometown. Mama begged and cried for help. The policeman took pity on us and pointed to the ghetto group, warning us not to get out of the line because the other group was going on a transport. I took Andy in my arms and covered him with a blanket to hide both our faces. This time I was lucky. Despite the inspections, I always turned the opposite way when a policeman passed and nobody noticed how young I was. Then we were ordered to walk. It was a long way through the city to the ghetto. I did not dare look back. It was horrible to hear those cries and moans. I knew they were being ordered to concentration camps. Most of them died there.

I'll tell you what the ghetto was like. It was several streets downtown bounded by Király and Dohány on the west and east and Károly Körút and Nagyatádi Szabó on the north and south. In between there were about ten streets. There was a wooden wall all around the ghetto and two gates where Arrow Cross men were standing guard. The non-Jewish population had moved out and moved into abandoned Jewish homes. They had lots of choices because we were concentrated fifteen to one room. Many Jewish homes and apartments were left vacant.

We were taken to 45 Akácfa utca. It was dark again. We went up to the fourth floor with about thirty people. We were dead tired, not only from walking but because Mama and I had taken turns carrying our sleeping Andy. We had to wait about two hours until the janitor opened the apartment on a police order. It was a two-bedroom apartment. Mama, my girlfriend Mary Csillag, whom I had met on the way, and I were the first to step in. Quickly we put our children on the couch. Four people slept on that couch for seven weeks. Other people found a place for themselves on the floor or in armchairs or in the two beds in the other room.

The ghetto's gate was open until December 10. I went out a few times when I had a chance to buy or ask for some food. Some of our friends were humane and gave me what they could spare. When they closed the gates, nobody was allowed to get in or out except the driver of a hearse. I felt like a mouse in a trap.

Andy became sick again. It seemed to be pneumonia. He grew pitifully thin, and there was no doctor or medicine. But God helped him. He got better. By that time, we had no food. We managed to get some meals for the first few weeks, but then less and less, and during the last two weeks we had only some flour, which Mama had saved. She mixed it with water, made some buns the size of my palms and baked them on the top of the little iron stove. Fortunately, there was some wood piled up in the pantry, so at least we were warm. Mama would not take one bite from those buns. It was useless to plead with her. She said, "I want you and the child to live for your husband. What will I tell him when he gets back and asks if I took good care of you?" Your mother was wonderful to us. I will never forget it.

On Christmas night an air raid started that was heavier than ever before. At first everybody thought the Arrow Cross would start to kill us with their machine guns. There were rumours that they wanted to massacre the Jews in the ghetto, but it wasn't that. The attacks lasted three or four days and nights. Huge bombs fell all over the city. When a big one fell just a few inches in front of the house, we got permission to move to the ground floor because of the small children. We got a very small room and thirteen of us moved in, including five children.

One day, a man opened the door and stepped in. Guess what, my dear? It was your father! He had escaped from Austria and had been taken to the ghetto by a policeman. He had gone door to door asking about us. Now we were all together, except you. A few days later our dear friend Tony, Andy's godfather, came in. I was so happy to see him, and when he gave me a piece of bread for Andy, I almost kissed his hand. The poor child was so hungry he begged for bread. He would show with his tiny fingers just how small a piece of bread he wanted.

But we had none. I was awfully hungry too and was often half asleep from hunger. In front of my eyes I always saw food. But I didn't care for myself. I only wanted Andy to get some food. When Tony saw us suffering from hunger, he promised that he would bring some bread no matter what. There was already block-to-block fighting in the city between the Germans and Soviets, and no civilians were permitted to go out on the streets.

We were days away from freedom, Tony told us. He comforted us and promised that in two days we were going to be free. He went out for the promised bread and never came back. Later I learned that a German soldier had killed him. I feel awful that he died because of me, because he wanted to bring food for us when he was not supposed to leave the house.

The next day, Thursday, January 18, 1945, I saw the first Soviet soldier in the yard. We were unimaginably happy. We were allowed to go home, but Papa couldn't. He was lying on the couch unconscious. I ran home as fast as my weak body could tolerate but our apartment was a mess. It had been occupied first by German soldiers, who had fled when the Soviets came, and then the Soviets had taken their place. I went to our superintendent and asked for some food. She gave me some bread, coffee, sugar, jam and a small bottle of milk. I ran back, out of breath. I was very weak but the joy of our freedom gave me strength. Besides, I was afraid Papa would die before he got any nourishment. Mama made coffee, and Papa, who came to life with the aid of a doctor, drank some of it. Then Mama fixed some lunch, which was heavenly – coffee with milk and sugar, and bread and jam. After I gave a piece of bread with jam on top of it to Andy, he was so happy that he was laughing, crying and jumping with joy all at the same time.

After lunch, we all went home. It seemed that we had just escaped from the throat of death. But our dear friend Tony hadn't lived to see this moment. And neither had many millions of Jews who had died from hunger, been shot to death, or who had been thrown into the icy water of the Danube, wounded first by gunshots. And then there were those who had been killed in the gas chambers. We suffered so much, but I know others suffered more. Much, much more!

The fate of my dear parents and two of my sisters and their families, I learned from a newspaper. The Jewish population of Pécs and its out-skirts had been taken away on July 4, 1944. The article described how they had been crowded into cattle wagons, seventy to eighty people in one car, without any food or drink. By the time they arrived in Ausch-witz after days of travelling, many of the people were already dead. In Auschwitz, they were sorted into groups, and children and the elder-ly, and also pregnant women, were put into gas chambers and then cremated.

After I read the article, I was sick to my stomach. Merciful God! Where were you? How did you let it happen? My poor old parents. They never hurt anybody. They were quiet and diligent, hard-working peo-ple. They had just started to have an easier life after all of us had gotten married.

While we were in the ghetto, I had a strong feeling that we would pull through that horrible time. I wanted to live for you! I want you back! You will come back, won't you dearest? I am waiting for you with all my heart and all my love.

Your loving wife, Ibi

As I wrote the letter, I felt strongly that Zolti would come home and that he was alive. And at that time, he was still alive – very sick, but alive.

Aftermath

While I was in the ghetto, and even after I was liberated, I never heard the name Raoul Wallenberg. It took a few years for me to learn who this man was and that I and many thousands of Hungarian Jews owed our lives to him. He was a Swedish diplomat whose name is almost legendary today, known not only by Hungarian Jews but by people all over the world.

Wallenberg was thirty-two when he accepted an offer to go to Hungary as the Swedish humanitarian attaché to the Swedish Legation in Budapest. After arriving in Budapest on July 9, 1944, he at first helped and saved only Swedish citizens. But later on, he helped groups in danger whether they were Swedish or not.

I heard that he was notified of the gathering of Jews at the Tattersall racetrack on October 16, 1944, and that it was due to his intervention that we were freed. Also, two days before the ghetto was liberated by the Soviets, Wallenberg learned from reliable sources of a plan to wipe out the ghetto by mines or machine guns. On January 16, 1945, Wallenberg was notified that some five hundred German soldiers and twenty-two Arrow Cross members had gathered in the Grand Hotel Royal and that they wanted two hundred Hungarian police to participate in the killing. They wanted to start that night.

Wallenberg, fearing for his life in the last days before the liberation, was in hiding. But one of his men, on Wallenberg's advice, asked for an audience with Gerhard Schmidhuber, a German general who was responsible for organizing the massacre. The man warned the general that Wallenberg would see to it that he would be tried as a murderer if he didn't stop this crime. The general then instructed all the people involved to abandon the plan. For forty-eight hours, the people of the ghetto were in the hands of God and only a miracle could have saved us. That miracle had happened, thanks to Wallenberg.

In April and May 1945, when the survivors started to come home after the war, I went to the railroad station every day. I met some of Zolti's comrades and, with a thumping heart and much hope, I asked about him. No one seemed to know anything about my husband. Finally, one comrade, Géza Klein, gave me a name and address, saying that this man had a list of those who had survived. The list was actually of those who had died, but he didn't have the heart to tell me. I ran home and told my in-laws that I was going to that address immediately.

On my way there, I bought some candy for my son, feeling hopeful and happy. Only when I reached the house did it hit me. I felt an awful sensation. When the man asked my relationship to Zolti, I told him that I was his sister. Then he told me that Zolti had died from typhus in February. I cried out, "No! It is not true! My husband promised me he would come home!" The comrade became very angry that I had not told him the truth about my relationship to Zolti. On my way home, I stuffed my handkerchief into my mouth so as not to cry out loud.

I didn't have to say anything to my in-laws. Seeing me, they knew what had happened. But they didn't believe it either. They took Andy and went to the address I had just been to. They thought that the man had been mistaken and had given me the wrong information. Unfortunately, he hadn't. The man told my in-laws the same thing – that Zolti had had typhus. He also told them that there was one comrade, Béla Boros, who had done everything he could to save Zolti's life.

Then the man told my in-laws what he hadn't told me – that the Germans had shot Zolti dead on February 18, 1945, because of his illness. Zolti would have been thirty-one that March. Mama and Papa didn't tell me about the shooting for a long time.

How I managed to live without my darling, I don't know. On the street, whenever I saw a tall young man coming toward me, I wouldn't look at his face so that I could pretend he was Zolti. I imagined him hugging me just as he used to. I played this game for a long time. Finally I had to face the truth: Zolti, my darling, my beloved husband, was gone and I had to accept the loss.

It was also in April 1945 that my sister Elizabeth walked through the door of our building. I didn't recognize her. Her hair was gone, she had had typhus, and she seemed not more than ninety pounds. After our emotional meeting, the first thing I did was put her into bed and feed her a little bit every two hours. After a long period of time, when she was strong enough to talk, I asked her to tell me her story.

On November 11, 1944, policemen had taken her from Aranka's bungalow. By that time, Aranka and her daughter were hiding with false papers. Elizabeth was taken to a sports field. From there, with thousands of other women, she had to walk to a brick factory. They arrived by night, and the next morning, for work, they walked to a village that was still part of Hungary. Their job was to dig ramparts miles and miles long. They were there for about three weeks. They had to get up every morning at 4:30 a.m. After they drank a cup of weak, black coffee, they started their half-hour walk, carrying their spades and hoes. Their lunch was some soup and a small piece of bread. When there was an air raid, they stopped working, knelt down in the rampart and prayed for a fast death by a bomb.

After about three weeks, the women had to march to the Hungarian-Austrian border, where the Germans took them into custody. By that time, many of the women had died. The survivors were taken to Lichtenwörth in Austria, to a huge empty factory that was part of the Mauthausen concentration camp. Their lives were unimaginable. The prisoners lay on rotten straw. There, nobody had to work. The German plan was to starve all three thousand women to death. It was almost successful. Only a few hundred survived.

On April 1, 1945, the Soviet army liberated the camps. Those who had enough strength started to walk home. Elizabeth had gotten typhus in the last few weeks, and she was too sick and weak to walk. She and many others stayed behind for some time. People opened the food storage cellar and took what they could. There was some sugar, jam and honey. Elizabeth crawled there on her hands and knees. If a woman had not taken pity on her, Elizabeth would not have received anything. She was given some sugar cubes and water.

After a few days, my sister started her journey home with two other women. They walked for two weeks. On their way, some people in the villages gave them food and shelter for the night in their barns. In one of the villages, they found an empty house; the occupants had fled from the Soviets. Four other women, who had arrived earlier, occupied the beds, so Elizabeth and her two companions lay on the floor. Somehow my sister had saved her good winter coat, and she put it on for cover, giving her blanket to the other two women.

After falling asleep, Elizabeth was suddenly awakened by a flashlight. A Soviet soldier stood above her, saying, "Burżuj" (Polish for "bourgeois") because he had seen her good coat. He pulled Elizabeth up by her hand, but she fell back when he released her. He asked, "What is wrong with you? Are you sick?" And then Elizabeth saved herself from a probable rape by saying the one word that came to her mind: "Syphilis." The Soviet jumped back. Elizabeth's quick thinking likely saved the rest of the women from being raped as well. The soldiers even gave them bread and a couple of rabbits that they had killed, which the women cooked and ate. The next day, Elizabeth and her companions continued their journey, boarding a train to Budapest.

Elizabeth stayed with us for a couple of weeks, and, with careful nursing and a doctor's care, she slowly regained her strength. Then she went to Aranka's home to stay for another few weeks. When she was strong enough, Elizabeth took a train to our hometown, Pécs, to see if anyone from her husband's family was alive. She found only a sister-in-law. Elizabeth's husband, his seventeen-year-old brother and her in-laws had all perished in Auschwitz.

Elizabeth stayed in Pécs with her sister-in-law for a year. During that time, she was introduced to a man named Feri (Frank) who had lost his wife and two sons in the Holocaust. Elizabeth and Frank married in 1946. Their only child, a son named Tomi, was born in 1948. They moved to Budapest the following year, and Frank worked as a cutter in a textile factory.

My sister Aranka had a different story. She managed to get false papers for herself and her daughter, Marianna, and flee to an organization run by nuns. It was a home primarily for young women who came to the capital from smaller cities to work but had no place to stay. They had to pay for their board. The food was meagre, with little variety. There were strict rules at the home. Men were not allowed to visit the women, and all the boarders had to be home by 9:00 p.m. each night.

Later, the nuns gave shelter to those who had been bombed out of their homes. Aranka said she was one of them. There were some Jews in hiding among the refugees, which the Mother Superior knew, but she didn't know that my sister and Marianna were also Jews. One day, my sister told me that the Mother Superior approached her and told her that both she and her daughter had to go to a priest for confession. Aranka replied that she had just confessed last month. "Then your little girl must do it," replied the nun. Her daughter asked, "Mommy, what can I say to the priest? What is a confession anyway?" Aranka told her to be calm and lie a little bit, to say that she had stolen an apple or hadn't told the truth about something.

"What will the priest say after I confess to those things?" she wanted to know. "He will say that he forgives you for your sins, and that is all."

Marianna did as she was told. When she came out from the chapel, she was so relieved that she started to laugh, and with dancing steps she went to her mother. Seeing this, the Mother Superior said angrily, "Aren't you ashamed of yourself? You just confessed and already you are laughing and dancing?" The poor child didn't know that she was not supposed to do these things after the confession.

The priest must have known that the girl was Jewish. On Christmas Day, he gave a beautiful sermon, during which he said, "Don't mind the enemies today. Love and humanity will keep us all together." Aranka and Marianna managed to stay at the home until the city was freed from the Germans, but there were fearful moments when Arrow Cross bandits or Germans went in to look for Jews in hiding. All of the Jews had false papers and the Mother Superior knew about most of them and defended them; they were left alone.

Aranka's husband, Jenö, had been sent to a concentration camp but escaped to the Soviets near the end of the war, and he was with the Soviets in Budapest when they liberated us on January 18, 1945.

I heard Margaret's story from her second husband, Joseph (Joe). Her first husband, Vilmos, had died in the early 1940s. He was buried in Pécs, and Margaret came to the cemetery from her village quite often to visit his grave. One day, as she was sitting on a bench in front of the tombstone, a man came over and politely asked her if he could sit down. They started to talk, and the man told Margaret that he had lost his wife not long before and that her tombstone was beside that of Margaret's husband. They talked about their spouses' illnesses and their deaths. The man, Joseph Halmos, was a gentile, but his wife had been Jewish, as was his teenaged son.

Margaret and Joe became friends and soon fell in love. After a time, Joe proposed to Margaret and she happily accepted. Unfortunately, there were already restrictive laws for Jews, and Joe, as a gentile, was not allowed to marry a Jew. On his advice, Margaret gave up her store and home and moved in with him. Joe had a grocery store on the outskirts of the city and an apartment behind the store. That period of time while they were together was the happiest in Margaret's life. Unfortunately, this happiness was short-lived.

Joe told me that when the Jewish population was rounded up for the ghetto, he jumped on his bicycle and escorted the group, which included Margaret, as far as he could. Then, hiding his tear-soaked face from the gendarmes, he watched as the Jews were herded into the ghetto. Joe's son, Tomi, who was only eighteen years old, had been taken away earlier to a forced labour camp. Neither he nor Margaret returned.

At the beginning of 1946, I went to Pécs with my son, Andy, to see what had happened to my father's shop. Joe invited us to stay in his home. To my chagrin, I learned that my father's shop had burned down. When and how it happened, I don't know. Andy and I stayed a few weeks there, because the fresh country air was good for a child. Besides, Andy liked Joe very much. They became good friends, and Joe loved my son.

Joe talked about Margaret a lot. He told me that when Margaret mentioned to Mother that she wanted to move in with him, Mother was at first very much against it but because of the circumstances, Mother reconsidered, and she even made a nice fish supper for their engagement.

Before I left for Budapest, Joe said to me, "Neither of us can live with the dead, my dear. Would you consider marrying me?" His question came as a big surprise, and initially I didn't know what to say. Then I gathered my thoughts and replied, "Sorry, Joseph, but first of all, the age difference between us is too great. [I was twenty-nine years old while Joe was forty-eight.] Second, I couldn't live in Pécs again. The memories of everything about the city are just too much for me. Also, I would feel uncomfortable marrying you when I know how much you and my sister loved each other and how happy she was with you." He understood and accepted my refusal. Still, when he came to visit us the next summer in Budapest, he told my in-laws how sorry he was that I had refused his proposal.

A year after I wrote that letter to my husband, I added a few more lines to it and addressed it to my young son.

Budapest, February 18, 1946
My dear little son, Andy,
You are a small boy yet, only three and a half years old. You were with us in that terrible time, but you didn't know what was happening. You did not know why you couldn't get a bite of bread when you were awfully hungry, and you don't know why you had no father. I wrote a letter to your daddy to tell him what had happened to us. I felt very strongly that he must come back to us. Since then, I have found out he will never come back because he was sick and the Germans shot him to death February 18, 1945, one year ago today. I still cry for him with painful tears, and I will cry until I am dead.

Now I will keep this letter for you because I want you to know what happened to us when you are old enough to understand. Be my good little boy always. God help me to raise you.

Your loving mother

I still treasure that letter written in Hungarian, together with some of Zolti's postcards from the labour camp. He always wrote that he loved his *kicsi Andriskám*, little Andriska, and me. On one of the cards, he congratulated Andy on his second birthday and he wrote, "I can't send anything but my love."

A Single Mother

I began to arrange my life without my husband. I started to work in a dressmaker's shop. The workers there were all young women, and two were wives of Zolti's comrades. We became friends. I lived with my in-laws, who actually wouldn't have let me go even if I could have afforded my own place, and Mama took care of Andy.

In the first few years after the war, if any man came to visit me and sat on the divan, Mama got upset. She said that nobody should sit on that couch, which had belonged to her son. Many men who had survived the camps had come back and discovered that their families were wiped out, and they wanted to marry and start new families. I was asked by a few in the first year after the war ended, but I wasn't ready to marry yet.

However, there was one young man, Paul, who came to visit my in-laws. He had been a friend of Zolti's in their hometown. He was tall and handsome and somehow reminded me of my darling husband. Eventually he confessed that he visited us to ask me to marry him, so I asked him, "Why do you want to marry a widow with a child when you could choose among many single girls?" "Because I was a friend of your husband's and I always liked you and I know that you had a good marriage," he answered. He wanted to move to the United States or Australia and take Andy and me with him. When I mentioned to Mama that maybe it would be a good idea to leave every bad thing behind and start a new life far away from home, Mama was upset and cried, "I know this man; he is a penny pincher and wouldn't give the child what he needs."

One day, Zolti's comrade Béla Boros came to visit me. He and his young wife had lived on the outskirts of Budapest. She had been taken away, pregnant, before she had time to escape to the city, where she had an aunt. She was killed in Auschwitz. Béla was so alone; he had nobody left in his family. He was short and not all that good-looking. His bushy and slightly curly hair seemed like it always needed a cut. His face was narrow, and his lower lip was thicker than the upper one, but his eyes, which were huge and blue like the water of our Lake Balaton, showed concern and understanding for people. Prior to his death, Zolti had written to me about how nice and good-hearted Béla was and even mentioned that if anything happened to him, Béla would take care of Andy and me.

After his first visit, Béla asked me if he could come to see us more often. Andy and Béla loved each other from the beginning. I told Béla I didn't want a boyfriend, and I added that maybe I never would. He said he just wanted to be with us as a friend. I agreed to this, and most of the time we took Andy with us on our outings. On our excursions, when Andy got tired, Béla carried him on his back. Béla spent more and more time with us, and he declared he was in love with me. In the summer of 1947, when Béla asked me to marry him, I told him to give me a few days to think it over. I asked my in-laws for their opinion. They didn't oppose the marriage because they knew how much Béla liked their grandson. After a few days, I told Béla I would marry him. He bought a gold wedding band, and we were engaged.

Béla seldom spoke about his wife and unborn child. All I know is that his wife had been a teacher, and, coincidentally, she had the same first name as me. However, I talked a lot about Zolti, and Béla was patient and understanding. Béla inherited his aunt's apartment, and we planned to move there after we got married. Our relationship was one-sided because I had no special emotional attachment to him.

I had accepted Béla's proposal because I felt lonely and was sure he would be a good father to Andy.

During our courtship, I quit my job as a dressmaker and went to work at an orphanage for Jewish children. I had always wanted to work with children. The orphanage was sponsored by the American Jewish Congress and was called the Louise Wise Home for Children. It was far away from the city, and I had to live there. Andy stayed with his grandparents and went to a nearby kindergarten.

The orphanage was comprised of two buildings at the edge of the Buda forest. The main centre was in the middle of about eighteen acres of a park, and the smaller building housed certain staff members who were required to live on the grounds. Some mornings, I got up early to walk in the rolling hills, marvelling at the huge pine trees and lovely flower beds, watching the sun rise and listening to the different birdsongs.

At the time of my arrival at the orphanage, the children had never been allowed to go outside the building, due to the doctor's orders. Maybe he was afraid that the children would get a disease if they were in contact with the outside world. I started to hint to the orphanage's managers that they should let the children outdoors. I didn't think it was healthy to completely isolate them, even though they had everything they needed inside.

There were roughly fifty or sixty children between the ages of three and nine years divided into different age groups. Most of them had only one relative – a parent, a grandparent, an aunt or a distant relative. Some had nobody at all. I took care of a group of girls between four and eight years old. I loved my girls. They sensed my feelings, and the children sought my love with every hug and touch they gave me. My work with them was more than a job and a much-needed salary. It gave me pleasure to perform good deeds. I took care of the children's physical needs and occupied the little ones while the older girls attended school in the home's classroom.

Every second Sunday, there were visiting hours, which caused great excitement among the children. Unfortunately, there were some who had no visitors, so the staff spent extra time with them. Before visiting day, I would bathe my girls and wash their hair. In the morning, I would give each of them a white pinafore to wear over her dress and white ribbons for her hair, which I had braided. All clean and beautiful and with shining eyes, they would then gather at the gate and wait for their visitors. I was gratified when I received compliments on the children's appearance and thanks for the good care and love I gave them.

I had only one day off a week to go home. Usually I left for my day off in the evening, after putting my girls to bed. After I tucked them in and kissed them goodnight, they would remind me not to forget to return with a treat for them, and I always did. Béla would be waiting for me at the bus station, and we either went to a movie or spent a quiet evening at his apartment listening to opera records. Around eleven o'clock, he would escort me home. By that time, my in-laws and Andy were in bed. Andy would have been in bed already even if I had gone straight home from the orphanage. By delaying my return, I could spend some time with my fiancé. Arriving home, I would tiptoe to my son's bed, kiss him gently and then go to my own bed. The following day I spent entirely with my son. On some Sundays, he and his grandparents visited me at the orphanage.

One day, I received good news from the principal of the orphanage. Finally, the doctor in charge of the children had given permission for them to go outdoors. "Children! Children!" I called, clapping my hands on a sunny Sunday morning. "I have great news for you. Guess what? We have received permission from Miss Éva to go for a picnic in the forest." I still remember the excitement. While the children went to their rooms to change, I went to the kitchen to ask the cook to fill a picnic basket with sandwiches and fruit for the children. I took the basket from the kitchen and went to meet the girls. I unlocked the gate, and for the first time we happily marched out together. The children laughed, chatted and sang as we walked. We didn't have to walk far to reach the forest, which was full of huge pine trees and blue, yellow, white and lilac wildflowers. The smells of the early summer hit me, and I inhaled them deeply.

After walking for some time, we came to a small glade. We stopped and I spread out a blanket. The girls played games and picked flowers. They were so excited when they saw a rabbit, a squirrel or a deer. After lunch, the girls picked some more wildflowers, and each carried a bouquet home to present to Miss Éva, the director of the home. After that first outing, we were allowed to take the mountain train to the city, and during the winter, we could toboggan down the hills, which I enjoyed as much as the children did.

In 1947, after working at the orphanage for about a year, I could no longer stand to be apart from my son. Because the management was afraid I would leave my job, they allowed Andy, who was then five years old, to come and live at the orphanage. He was put in a different group from mine, and instead of calling me Mother, he had to address me by my first name. I understood and went along with this demand.

Of all my girls, I remember Ágnes (Ági) best. She was seven years old, with shiny black hair, big brown eyes and a narrow face with just a sprinkling of freckles. Ági limped slightly and rarely smiled. Those beautiful brown eyes were sad most of the time. She wanted so much to be loved. Her parents had been killed in the Holocaust. Ági had only a grandmother and a developmentally delayed aunt who lived together.

My sister Aranka and her husband, who had only one child and couldn't have any more, wanted to adopt. When I mentioned the children in the orphanage, they decided to come to see them. From the moment they saw Ági, they liked her. After obtaining permission, they took Ági home on weekends. Ági was happy and liked her parents-to-be so very much that she asked if she could call them Mother and Father.

After Ági had lived with Aranka, Jenö and their daughter, Marianna, for about three months, Ági's grandmother agreed to let them adopt her. Ági attended school near their home and was eager to make the arrangement permanent. Marianna was thirteen or fourteen years old at that time, and she, too, liked her little sister-to-be.

One day, Ági's grandmother came over to take her granddaughter home for a visit. Only Marianna was at home at the time, and the grandmother asked her to put a special dress on Ági. Marianna refused, saying that the dress had to be saved for school the next day. The grandmother got very angry and took the child and all her belongings back to the orphanage. When Aranka and Jenö got home and learned what had happened, they went to get Ági back. However, the old woman seemed to have completely changed her mind about the adoption. Ági was heartbroken. Aranka took her to their home a few more times to visit, but whenever the time came to return to the orphanage, Ági became sadder and more withdrawn than ever. How unfortunate it was to deprive a child of a loving family because of an old woman's spite.

When Andy reached school age, I left my job at the orphanage and got another job in a private kindergarten in the city so I could go home daily. Andy went to a nearby elementary school, and his teachers liked him very much. Despite the awful things he had been through, he was a kind, lovable child. He resembled his father, with the same wide forehead and narrowing face, although unlike his father, Andy had green eyes, and his hair was lighter and straighter. I always dressed him nicely so he never had to be ashamed of his looks, as I had been when I was a child. Zolti had wanted our son to be an athlete, as he was, so Andy was taught many sports. By the age of five, he was already able to swim, skate and ride a bicycle. He loved swimming best, and he still does.

Living with my in-laws, I felt that I wasn't a grown-up. Mama and Papa helped Andy and me in every way they could, but they prevented me from being independent. I wished for even one single room somewhere separate from them, where I could be on my own with my son. I knew that wish would never come true as long as I stayed in Hungary. When I applied to the government for an apartment of my own, the communist authorities told me that I had a roof over my head and that I should be satisfied with it.

Béla was not in a hurry to get married. He had been talking about leaving the country, and I think he was afraid of the responsibility of taking us with him. His plan was to escape alone to Vienna and then send for Andy and me. Together, we would go to Israel.

In the summer of 1948, Béla finally got the opportunity to leave Hungary. He promised that he would send for Andy and me as soon as he was able. Papa, who worked in one of the spas, did not know of this plan, which was a good thing. He had had to join the Communist Party, as did many Hungarian citizens after the war, and the Party was against anyone leaving the country. Papa had become a true communist, attending seminars and giving lectures about communism.

Many months later, a peasant woman knocked on our door with a note from Béla, in which he set a date for us to accompany this woman out of the country. Fortunately, Papa was not home when the woman came. I told the plan to Mama, and she didn't object. We kept the plan from Papa because, being a communist at that time, he would never have agreed to let us go.

The First Escape

One bright and mild October day in 1949, Andy and I went to the railway station where I was to meet the peasant woman who was our escape escort and another couple who also wanted to escape. Mama came with Andy and me. How hard it had been for her, knowing our intentions and having to hide her feelings. But she was strong. Mama even got on the train and accompanied us for a short while. Then she kissed us, wished us luck and got off the train at the first stop.

The other couple and the peasant woman were sitting in different rows from us. I kept an eye on the woman so we would know where to get off the train. After disembarking, we went to her home in a village near the Czechoslovakian border, where we had to wait until dark. I thought it was time to explain the situation to my son. I told Andy we were going to another country to meet Uncle Béla, who would become his new daddy. I explained that we had to be very quiet and careful because if the border guards captured us, they would put us in jail. Andy, who was six years old at the time, seemed to understand and was very co-operative.

After dark, we continued our journey on foot, often uphill. After a couple of hours, Andy whispered, "Mommy, I'm very tired. Let's take a rest now." "Please, darling, don't sit down," I replied. "If you sit down, we will get lost because we will lose the others." My son wanted to be brave, so he walked some more. But after another hour, he couldn't go any farther. I told our escort that Andy couldn't keep up. The woman then hoisted him onto her back and continued walking. It was only a minute before Andy fell asleep.

I was also very tired, and the knapsack on my back was getting heavier by the minute. I thought how nice it would be to leave my heavy burden behind, but I couldn't do that because the knapsack contained some basic necessities: a change of clothes for both of us, an extra pair of socks, some toiletries and two towels. Not even a toy for my son.

As we walked, I said a silent prayer. "Dear God, please let us reach the border safely. Let us start a new life in a free country. I don't have to tell you how much we suffered from our fellow Hungarians, how they hunted us like animals. You saved my son's life when he was a very sick baby in the ghetto, and I'm thankful for it even if you let my young husband be killed. Please, save us again, my God."

This time, however, my prayer went unanswered. Suddenly I saw a bright flash in the dark, and a voice yelled, "Stop or I will shoot!" We had been caught by the Czechoslovakian border guards. We were so close, so very close to freedom. Our escort, with Andy on her back, disappeared behind a hill. The rest of us stopped. Then, not seeing my son, I ran after her screaming, "Stop! Bring my child back!" Finally, the woman, carrying Andy, came back to us.

The border guards took us to their barracks. Much later, I was informed that there was an arrangement between the border guards and the peasant woman to capture everyone she took to the border. She was a traitor. We were exhausted by the time we arrived at the barracks. There, we were searched and almost all my money and valuables were taken. There wasn't much, but it was everything that I had. I had hidden the money in a variety of places – under the wrapper of a chocolate bar and inside the lining of my purse. The guards found all except two 100-forint bills.

In the barracks office, one guard offered his own cot for Andy and me. The couple lay on the floor. Andy slept through the night, but I stayed awake, wondering what the morning would bring. The next day, two guards took us back to the Hungarian border on foot. The Hungarian border guards locked us in the detention centre of their military station. Andy and I were in a different room from the others. For a few days, nothing happened. We got the same food as the soldiers and one straw mattress, on which Andy and I both slept. The guards allowed us out into the building's yard for one hour every day. I begged the guard to let my son stay out a little longer. When our time was up, my poor child never wanted to go back to the cell. The guard refused my request.

One day, Andy picked up two small stones in the yard. Later he whispered in my ear that the next time we returned to our cell, he would put the two stones under the door so that it could not be locked. My heart ached for my son. The only pastime that Andy had in the cell was cutting paper airplanes with my manicure scissors. When the guard saw this through the peephole, he came in and demanded the scissors from Andy. I don't know how it happened, but the small scissors disappeared before our eyes. When Andy refused to give them to the guard, he got really angry and threatened to spank my child. I asked my son to give the scissors to me. "Okay," he said, "but Uncle Guard has to turn his back to me." The guard was co-operative, and Andy pulled the scissors out from under his shirt. "What can I do all day now, Mommy?" he asked.

The cell had a very small window close to the ceiling. We carried the mattress to a place under the window and leaned it lengthwise against the wall. Then we climbed up and sat on the windowsill to look out at the street. The military barracks was on the outskirts of the city, so the street was not a busy one. There were sidewalks bordered by acacia, the national trees of Hungary. We were not able to see many passersby, but at least we were a bit occupied counting the few cars and pedestrians.

I had written a note, and I waited for the right moment, for somebody to notice us so that I could throw it down to them. In the note,

I asked that the recipient go to the Jewish Congress and ask them to notify my in-laws in Budapest about our whereabouts and to come for their grandson. Eventually, a young man, pushing his bicycle, noticed my frantic waving of the piece of paper. He stopped and bent down, pretending to fix his bicycle. Then he looked up and signalled. I threw the note. He picked it up, jumped on his bike and left.

Another two days passed. We were at the window again when I saw a woman approaching on the opposite side of the street. She looked familiar. Andy saw her, too. I had no time to finish my sentence, "Look Andy, that woman looks like your..." when my son yelled at the top of his voice, "Grandmama!" Mama looked up and motioned that we should be silent. Her face expressed a sadness that I would never forget. Later she told us that the Jewish Congress had notified her and Papa to come immediately for their grandson. My mother-in-law came with a man from the Congress and she waited outside while he went in.

Before they let Andy go home with his grandmother, the major of the guards asked my son to step into the office. I don't know what the conversation was between them; however, the major later told me that had it been within his power, he would have set us both free. The officer congratulated my son for being such a bright young fellow.

Andy was still in the office when Mama was called in for questioning. Earlier, I had informed Andy that two 100-forint bills were sewn into his coat cuffs. My instructions to him were that only when he and Grandma were safely out of the building could he tell her about the money. As soon as my mother-in-law stepped into the major's office, Andy said, "Grandma, when we are out on the street and alone, I will tell you a secret." The major was decent enough not to ask Andy about his secret.

I felt better knowing that Andy was going home and back to school, but I was concerned about my future. I was going to be punished for the crime of attempting to leave my country, where we had suffered so much. All I wanted was a peaceful life for me and my son.

The next evening, I was transferred from the military station to the jail in the nearest city, Miskolc. When I arrived, I was put in a small cell, where two women were lying on narrow cots. After the door was locked behind me, I stood there feeling very faint. Every night when I was a child, my mother had read the newspaper out loud to the family, and the word "jail" was often mentioned. I had had many dreams that I was in jail and awakened terrified that jail would be my destiny. Now, there I was; my childhood nightmares had become a reality.

As I stood in shock in the semi-darkness, unable to move or even cry, I felt a gentle hand on my shoulder. One of the women led me to her cot with an offer to share it with me. I thanked her for her kindness and accepted. Weeks later, I heard a rumour that she was a murderer.

The next morning, I was transferred into a larger cell, but it was still far too small for all the prisoners in it. All the women were Jewish dissidents. I don't remember how many beds were pushed together, but during the night, when one of us had to turn over, the entire row turned; otherwise we would not have had enough room. There was only one separate bed in a corner, in case somebody got sick. In the other corner of the cell, there was a pail to be used as a toilet. We managed to hang a bed sheet around it for some privacy. There were also a couple of basins for washing ourselves and our laundry.

Every day, we were required to go to the yard and walk in circles for one hour. Two female guards were appointed to watch us. One was malicious, with a bad temper, but the other was not so bad. We were forbidden to speak to one another. But the old-time prisoners always managed to exchange news or little written notes. I recognized the peasant woman who had betrayed us, and I cursed her in my thoughts, but I didn't make a scene. I was satisfied when I heard a rumour that she was sentenced to one year in prison. Later, however, I learned that the woman, being an informer, spent only a few days in prison and then was set free.

I didn't like to go outside, because there were often altercations among the prisoners. One day, a woman ran from the circle and jumped on another woman screaming, "You pig, you dirty pig! I'm here because of you! Because you denounced me!" She started to hit the woman, and their argument escalated into a big fist fight. The guards ran over and took the attacker away.

It was not expected that we work, the way long-term inmates did. We tried to create a routine for ourselves. In the mornings, we took one of the grey blankets that we used to cover ourselves during the night and spread it on the floor. We appointed one of the women as our gymnastics teacher. We stripped down to our panties and bras and did some exercises. All participated except two elderly women. We exercised for about thirty minutes a day, not caring that some of the male guards sometimes watched us through the peephole. We learned of their spying on us from a male dissident whose mother was in with us. The men's cells were across from ours in the same corridor.

We took turns doing our own laundry. The jail had a library, so we at least had some books to read. Everyone had the privilege of getting kosher food for lunch from the Jewish Congress. That lunch, which was much better food than that provided by the jail, was the highlight of our day.

The lights were shut off at 9:00 p.m., which made the nights very long, since no one could fall asleep that early. We talked in the dark and made a rule that only one person could speak at a time on any subject of her choosing. We talked about our homes, our plans for the future, our escapes, how we were caught, our families and our favourite foods. None of us talked about our experiences during the Holocaust, experiences that were still too vivid and painful.

My trial date eventually arrived. I was convicted and sentenced to six months of jail. I could not imagine having to stay so long. My lawyer, hired by the Jewish Congress, advised me to appeal. The Congress even deposited some money at the lawyer's office to be given to me when I was released.

Back in jail, I became ill. I had a constantly high fever, and the jail's doctor couldn't figure out the cause. He sent me to the hospital for an X-ray, and I had to walk there, together with some male prisoners and guards. Among the men were some dissidents, but they were handcuffed like criminals. I was glad that I wasn't handcuffed, because even though no one knew me in this strange city, I would have felt terribly embarrassed. The X-ray didn't show anything wrong. Back in jail, the doctor gave me a thermometer and instructed me to take my temperature three times a day. The malicious guard was supposed to check it every time. She never did.

Shortly after this, my second trial came up. One of my cellmates lent me her coat for this occasion. She was my height, but much heavier. The coat was light brown and made of good-quality camel's hair, which was soft and warm. It was big enough to wrap around me. The purpose of her lending me the large coat was to show how much weight I had lost. The judge must have known about my illness, because he asked me if it was true that I had a constantly high temperature. "Yes, your honour," I replied. Then he asked the guard if she had checked my temperature, as ordered. For a second, there was a strained silence. The guard knew that she hadn't done her duty. Finally, the guard said, "Yes, I checked it daily, and she has had a fever for weeks." This was probably the reason that my sentence was reduced from six months to three.

More than half of my sentence was already over, and I was counting the days until my release. One of the female guards started to crochet a huge tablecloth and gave it to us to work on. All of my cellmates participated because this made the time go by faster.

On one occasion, a friend of mine, whose husband had been a comrade of Zolti's, sent a beautiful parcel of sweets for me. The guard came in and showed me the contents of the parcel: chocolate, candies, cookies and homemade pastries. I craved sweets. The pastries were ones that Hungarians baked around Christmas time; one loaf was filled with poppy seeds and the other with walnuts and raisins.

Then the guard took the parcel away without giving me a single bite. I almost cried. She said that they would give it to the younger prisoners, but she lied. We had a young girl among us, and she didn't receive any of the sweets either.

Of course, I thought constantly about my son, Andy. I recalled how brave he had been during our attempted escape and in the detention centre. I imagined my reunion with Andy every day. I wondered what he was doing. Was he with his friends or had his grandpa taken him skating? Was he missing me? I hoped that he wasn't sick. I knew that he was in the best of hands with his grandparents, but I still missed him very much.

Light of My Eyes

The time for which I had been impatiently waiting arrived at last. I even got out a few days early, on December 18, 1950, because it was Stalin's birthday. Since Hungary was under Soviet occupation, the government celebrated the "great" leader's birthday by releasing political prisoners.

I hugged my cellmates and warmly thanked the sixteen-year-old girl who had done my laundry while I was sick. After I received documentation for my release at the office, a guard escorted me to the gate. I stepped out, and for a few seconds I stood there inhaling the crisp air of winter. How beautiful it was to be free again! I wanted to cry out to passersby, "I am free! I can go home to my little boy!"

First I went to my lawyer's office, where I received the money deposited by the Jewish Congress. Then I went to find a grocery store and bought white bread and a big chocolate bar. I ate them on the street, alternating between one bite of bread and one bite of chocolate. I went to the train station to make inquiries about the train leaving for Budapest and bought a ticket for the express train, which stopped only two or three times instead of at every village. I had to wait a couple of hours for this train, so I bought a newspaper to read. It was full of news about the celebrations for Stalin's birthday.

Finally, I heard the train's whistle. It stopped at the station just long enough for me to get on. As the train picked up speed, the click-clack of the wheels seemed to say, "I'm going home, I'm going home."

Two and a half hours later, I arrived at the Keleti railway station in Budapest, which was only a twenty-minute walk from my home. I ran all the way on the familiar streets and took a shortcut through the park where Andy played with his friends every day. I walked into our apartment building through the short, half-dark corridor to the yard. When I stepped in, there were my son and his grandma, eating their supper at the table.

They looked up, and my son leapt off his chair, crying out, "Mommy! Mommy! You're home!" I bent down, and as we hugged, he squeezed my neck so hard that he almost choked me. I held him and felt that he was the only person in the whole world who belonged to me. At that moment, I remembered Zolti's words when I had cried upon learning that I was pregnant during that terrible time: "Don't cry, darling. We need this baby. You will see."

Andy looked a little bit taller, and his greyish-green eyes were shining with happiness. His soft, light-brown hair was parted at the side and fell onto his forehead as usual, and he brushed it back with one of his hands. He was neatly dressed and clean, as he always had been.

Mama waited patiently for her turn to welcome me. After we exchanged some kisses, her first words were, "Are you hungry?"

"Yes, Mama, I'm starving," I answered. I looked around the familiar kitchen while Mama put a place setting on the table and served me some soup. I looked at the worn-out, pale-green furniture and the small wood- or coal-burning stove. I glanced up and saw the laundry drying on the clothesline, which hung just under the unusually high ceiling.

"Where is Papa?" I asked.

"He will be home soon. He had to go to a seminar," she replied. "You know, those political ones."

As I was saying, "I hope Papa forgives me," he stepped through the door.

His face showed only surprise, and he said coldly, "You are home, finally. If I hear that you try to escape from the country again, I, personally, will report you to the authorities." At the time, he believed that much in the communist government. I found out that I had been very lucky. People who tried to escape only a couple of weeks later than us were convicted and sentenced to years in prison with no appeal.

I corresponded with my fiancé, Béla, in Vienna. When he learned about our unsuccessful escape attempt, he wanted us to try again. I wrote to him that I wouldn't do it unless I got legal permission to leave the country. I applied every year and was rejected every time. Once a clerk even told me that I should call my fiancé back to let him know we weren't joining him. Béla waited for us for one and a half years, and then he went to Israel by himself.

~

Andy was a bit spoiled by his grandmother and was sometimes smart-alecky to her. Once, after some smart remark of his, she warned him, "If you don't behave, I'm going to get a job and you will be all alone." Andy apologized every time that he had been rude to her, but he would soon forget his promise to behave. Of course, his grandmother forgave him every time, as she always did. Andy was, as she called him, the "light of my eyes."

Mama stayed home to take care of Andy until he was eight years old. After that, she decided that she would go to work so she could contribute some money to the household. She took a job as a cook for a well-known family who were members of the Jewish Congress. Andy had to be on his own, so he wore a key to the apartment on a chain around his neck. At lunchtime, which was the main meal in Hungary, he walked home from school and warmed up his lunch. Andy was in Grade 1 when, on Mother's Day, he presented me with an envelope. In the envelope was a large card with Andy's photograph in the middle. His hair was pinned back with a bobby pin so that it wouldn't fall onto his forehead. He wore a navy-blue sweater over his white shirt, and he smiled slightly. Across the top of the card, he had printed in red letters, "To my dear mother." A small red heart was attached to the card with a red string. A piece of paper was also in the envelope with some flowers drawn by Andy, and he wrote the following on it, which I still treasure.

For my dear mother on Mother's Day. I wish you a very happy day from the bottom of my heart on this day. I also promise that I will not be rude to Grandma ever again.
Many kisses from your loving son,
Andy

~

When Andy was in Grade 2, he had a hard time with mathematics. I tutored him every day, and I learned the multiplication table well, but Andy had difficulty remembering the numbers. He was a good student, and usually after he read something only once, he could recite it back, but somehow he couldn't do this with numbers. At that time, I saw an advertisement in the newspaper for a position as a cashier. I needed a job, and I had already tried to go back to the kindergarten I had last worked in, but, to my surprise, they wouldn't hire me because I had tried to flee the country. So I had to look for something else. Almost all the stores were in the hands of the communist government. Only a few were privately owned and operated.

The ad was for a nationalized hardware store, and I went to apply. During my interview with the head bookkeeper, he asked me some questions about the multiplication table and saw how adept I was. "How do you know this subject so well?" he asked me in surprise. "Usually, ladies are not very good with the multiplication table." When I told him that I had to study it with my son, he laughed and hired me.

For the first couple of years, I was a substitute cashier. I had to go to different stores to replace the regular cashiers who were either sick or on vacation. I also had to do the bookkeeping for all the stores. I did not have an adding machine, and I had to add long columns of numbers. I was rewarded a few times for my good work. During this period, we also had to attend political seminars, but I did not become a member of the Communist Party.

Andy behaved better with his grandfather than he did with his grandmother. He adored his grandpa. Almost every night, his grandpa, who usually went to bed early, let Andy lie beside him and told him stories. These made-up stories were about a huge ship on which Andy was the captain and got involved in many adventures and a lot of mischief. Papa also took him skating and swimming and to many sporting events.

In the summer, my father-in-law was the director of a beautiful, huge outdoor swimming arena called Palatinus. It was built on Margaret Island, on the Danube River. Budapest had many outdoor pools with natural mineral water, but not all of them were as large as Palatinus. The arena had different pools – one with cool water, another with warm mineral water, and one with artificial waves. Every hour, a bell sounded, signalling that the artificial waves were coming up. Andy was allowed to ring the bell by pulling on its rope, and was very proud to have such an important job. At the sound of the bell, the whole crowd would run in the direction of the special pool, where they jumped in the waves. Around the poolside were grass, benches, snack bars, restaurants and souvenir shops. It was a favourite place not only for locals but for tourists as well.

Throughout these years, I continued to correspond with Béla in Israel. He never married. I felt so alone, and it seemed that all the decent men had married. I missed Béla. I still wasn't in love with him, but he was a good human being who had treated Andy and me very well.

Some summers, I spent my two-week vacation with Andy at a resort owned by the organization for which I worked. The resort, on a bank of the Danube River, was comprised of a couple of long buildings and small, separate cottages. There was a common dining room where guests ate their meals. The rent that the management of my hardware store asked for was very reasonable.

One summer, I pretended that our little cabin was my own apartment, which I didn't have to share with anybody but my son. We swam a lot, sunbathed and went to the nightly entertainment provided by the management. I made friends with some of my colleagues there, and Andy, who was then eleven or twelve, also found friends in his age group.

One afternoon, my son came to me and said in a low voice, "Mother, promise me that you won't punish me for what I did."

"What did you do, Andy? Why do you deserve punishment?" I asked.

"I swam across the Danube," he told me.

"Oh, my God! That was very dangerous! Who was with you?" I asked.

"Nobody."

Even adults did not dare to swim across the wide, fast-flowing river without an escort. As I had promised, I didn't punish Andy. I was glad no harm had come to him. After Andy swam across the Danube alone, he promised me he would not do any more wild things.

At the end of the vacation, we went back to our daily routines. Andy, in addition to school, went swimming every day. He was a good swimmer and was training for the next Olympics. Occasionally, he went twice a day to practise, early in the morning before school started and after school. Sometimes, when it was a cold winter day and I didn't want him to go, I didn't wake him in the morning. Still, Andy would wake himself up and hurry off to his training.

At that time, I was working steadily at one store on Rákóczi utca, a main street in Budapest that was a short distance from our apartment. One day, a friend of the store manager's came in. He introduced himself to me as Emil and said a few words. After the store closed, I found him waiting for me outside. He asked if he could walk me home. I agreed.

After that, Emil came to the store often and courted me. He told me he was divorced. He seemed sharp, and he was highly educated. Much later, I found out that Emil was a gambler. He went to the race-track every time he had a couple of forints to spend. When he won, he showered me with presents; however, sometimes he borrowed money from me.

On one cold winter day when we met after the store closed, Emil wasn't wearing a winter coat. He had sold it to get some money for his bad habit. My in-laws knew about our friendship and were strongly against it. Sometimes I didn't see Emil for months, and then he would unexpectedly show up again. One day, he asked me to marry him. I hesitated. Although I was lonely and longed for my own home and family life, Emil didn't have a steady job, and he was a gambler. On top of that, he and Andy hated each other. I refused his proposal, but we continued to date for a while.

The Second Escape

On the warm afternoon of October 23, 1956, from inside the store, we heard singing and marching coming from the streets. We all hurried outside to investigate. The marchers in the street were university students who had started a peaceful demonstration against the Soviets. Hungary had been under Soviet occupation since World War II, and the people of Hungary were fed up and wanted freedom. By evening, the crowd had become much larger. Like an avalanche, the protests got uglier and more violent as the days went by. The protesters stole as many weapons as they could, and some opened the gates of the jails.

Then the mob started to target Jews. I saw posters saying, "You Jews don't have to go to Auschwitz. We will kill you right here." Hardly ten years had passed since the war, when Jews had been killed by the millions. After such a horrific tragedy, Hungarians were again threatening Jews. But no, not again! I wouldn't let them do what they had done to us in 1944 during World War II.

The attempted revolution went on and on until troops from the Soviet Union invaded to defeat it. The Soviets' tanks were soon roaming the streets. Some Hungarian youths – as young as twelve and thirteen – made Molotov cocktails and threw them at the tanks. My in-laws and I had a hard time keeping Andy in the house. He wanted to go out to meet his friends; God knows what he wanted to do.

One day, two young Soviet soldiers who weren't more than eighteen years old came to our apartment. We were on the ground level and our door was the first in the courtyard. The soldiers asked for some water. Fortunately Papa, who spoke several languages, including Russian, understood what they wanted and gave them a few glasses of water to drink. The two soldiers were so frightened at first; they had poked their rifles into the open door before they entered. I actually felt very sorry for them.

Another day, Andy and some other children from the building were playing in the yard, collecting empty shell cartridges from the ground. Some Soviet soldiers came in, and because Andy was the tallest of the boys, one of the soldiers addressed him. I saw the incident through the window and thought that they were only talking. Andy knew some Russian because it was a compulsory subject in his school. He told me later that the soldiers saw the cartridges in his hand and therefore wanted to take him away. But when he showed them that the cartridges were empty and explained that he was only playing with the other children, they let him go.

The whole country was in turmoil. The beautiful city of Budapest was in ruins once more. There was no electricity for days, and the stores were closed. People broke into the stores and plundered the city. I couldn't go to work for a week or so. It was not safe to be on the streets.

In the first week of November, the Soviets defeated the uprising. People started to escape from the country, and we all listened to their messages on Radio Free Europe. They encouraged their friends and relatives to follow them. Those messages encouraged me, too, to leave. This time, my in-laws both agreed. Papa, who had once threatened to report me if I ever tried to escape again, now said, "Go, my daughter. Go anywhere you can. Just far away from here." He had become bitterly disappointed in the Communist Party. Mama also approved of my plan, but she was crying as she asked, "Will I see my grandson, the light of my eyes, ever again?" "Yes, Mama, you will," I replied as I hugged her, almost crying myself.

On a cold November night, I approached my son to ask him, "What would you say, Andy, if I said let's go to the West and start a new life?"

"Are you serious, Mother?" he asked me. "You want me to leave my friends, school, teachers, swim training and grandparents behind?"

"Yes, my dear. If you want to come with me, you will have to do all those things. But I won't force you."

"All right, Mother, but why? Why do you want to leave our country?" he asked.

I pulled my son close to me, put my arms around his shoulders and explained to him, "During the war, you were only two years old. We were lucky to be taken to the ghetto, even though many of us died of hunger and sickness or by shooting. You were near death because you were very ill and there was no doctor, no medicine and no food. And all those things happened to us because we are Jews. You also know that is the reason your daddy was killed. Right now, we are in the midst of a revolution, and I don't want the same thing to happen to us again. Now we have our chance to escape and to start a new and peaceful life somewhere else."

Andy was convinced. As a matter of fact, it was a big adventure for him and he got very excited. But there were a couple of worrisome questions remaining: how and with whom could I escape? I arranged a meeting with Emil, and I mentioned my plan to him and asked for his help and advice. As a dissident, he also wanted to leave; time was running out, and it would soon be difficult to flee. He told me where to go.

In the last week of November 1956, Andy and I said goodbye to Mama and Papa. I told them that we were going to join a group, but I didn't mention that Emil was among it. I was too busy with my own problems to even think of the heartache and sorrow Mama and Papa must have been feeling when their beloved and only grandchild and I left forever.

Much later, I found a box of old letters dating back to 1957. There were letters from my old fiancé, Béla; one of my girlfriends; Andy's favourite teacher, a young woman named Márta Beke; a cousin on my father's side; my sister Elizabeth, and Papa. Elizabeth's letter was a long one, and among many things she wrote this:

I went to see your in-laws today. It was terrible to see your Papa crying in his bed and Mama sitting in the corner on her favourite little stool crying her heart out. I went to kiss and comfort them. I told them that you both are all right and that is what all of you wanted, a safer and better future. I promised to see them often. They calmed down a little, and Papa told me in a shaking voice that if they had been younger, they would have gone with you and Andy.

We met the group in the Keleti railway station to go by train to Vienna. We boarded one train but had to change to another train to Vienna after a few hours. Before we could board the second train, we were captured by the Soviets. At the station, the group was split up into twos and threes. Andy, Emil and I were sitting on a bench when two Soviet soldiers came over. When they asked where we were going, Andy told them that we were going to visit relatives in Vienna. They didn't believe this and ordered us to return to Budapest. Luckily they didn't arrest us, and when we promised to go back, they left us alone.

We didn't return to Budapest; instead, we hid in a small hotel and tried again the next morning. This time, we were lucky. After many kilometres on foot and a long train ride, we arrived in Vienna. When our little group got off the train, it was night and we didn't know where to go, so we walked up to the first police officer we saw and informed him that we were Hungarian refugees. He took us to the nearest police station and put us in a cell for the night. Being in jail again brought back unpleasant memories for me, but I knew that it was different this time because the police were only providing shelter for the night.

The next morning, we went to the authorities, where we were registered and given assistance. They placed us in hotels and displaced persons camps and gave us money, food and transportation passes. We were helped by the Jewish Congress in Vienna as well. During our four weeks in Vienna, Andy had a good time exploring the city.

Papa had a brother-in-law, Karl, in Vienna and had given us his address just in case. Karl was a bitter old man who still mourned the loss of his only child, a ten-year-old daughter, and his wife, who had been taken to Auschwitz and killed. Karl's wife had been Papa's only sister. I saw Karl only once, but Andy spent a lot of time with him and ate lunch or supper with him almost every day. We also went to see a schoolmate of Mama's, Elsa, and she too was nice to us.

In contrast to Budapest, which was in darkness and ruins when we left, Vienna was gorgeous and full of light, beautiful buildings and friendly people. I felt so emancipated, so happy. It seemed as if I was just starting to live again without fear.

We encountered many kind people during our time in Vienna. On occasion, we would need a small household item, and when the storeowner learned that we were refugees, he would give it to us for free. One day, Andy and I were walking along a sidewalk eating doughnuts when a police officer greeted us from his post in the middle of the road with a loud "Guten Appetit!" I shouted back, "Danke schön!" (Thank you!) A few days before Christmas, I saw another police officer directing traffic from a small platform in the middle of the road. Around his feet was a pile of gifts that he had received from drivers who passed him daily.

Like most of our fellow refugees, we wanted to go to the United States. We spent an entire night in front of the United States embassy in Vienna waiting for admittance, but to no avail. Only those who had relatives in the States were able to emigrate there. When we heard that Canada would take us, we applied.

On December 27, 1956, Andy, Emil and I set sail on a huge ship called the MS *Berlin*. It was a luxury ship with some two thousand passengers, including two hundred Hungarians. Andy enjoyed the journey, participating in sports activities such as swimming and tennis, but I was seasick most of the time. We were at sea for eleven days, arriving in Halifax on January 7, 1957. I still have our tickets, which cost the Canadian government $175 each.

We arrived in Halifax in the morning and were escorted to Immigration Hall, where each of us two hundred Hungarians were given a paper shopping bag with a handle, something we didn't have at home. (Since paper was very precious in Hungary, we usually took our own cloth bags when we went shopping.) Each of the paper shopping bags contained necessities such as a towel, toothbrush and soap. We also got five dollars each, the first Canadian money I had ever seen.

After having coffee and doughnuts, we were taken into a room for a medical examination and X-rays. I didn't see much of Halifax, only some deep snow and workers with unusually heavy boots. On the same day, we boarded a train for Winnipeg. People who had relatives in Montreal and Toronto were allowed to go there; the rest of us were assigned a destination.

This was the first time that we had travelled in a train with sleeping facilities. We were fascinated when, at night, a porter made our seats into couches on which we could sleep. He also put covers on them for us. It was also the first time that I felt at a loss due to my lack of knowledge of English; until this point, we had always had a Hungarian interpreter.

A Place of Our Own

Seventy-two hours later, we arrived in Winnipeg, our destination in our adopted country. The temperature was -40°C. We had never experienced such cold and we were shivering in our thin coats and shoes. However, we once again experienced the kindness of strangers, people from the Jewish Child and Family Service, who supplied us with warm clothes and many other needed items.

We stayed in Immigration Hall in Winnipeg for three weeks. The government officials served us white sandwich bread, which tasted like pastry, with our meals, and I began to despair that Canada had any other type of bread. While still in Immigration Hall, we began to learn English. I was motivated to learn the language. I felt so helpless without it.

One bright, sunny day, my son asked my permission to go outdoors. When I told him to put on his cap, he protested that it was sunny outside. "I know it looks gorgeous, but it is awfully cold," I reminded him. Andy put on only his thin coat and ran out of the building. In five minutes, he was back inside – both his ears were frozen, and his hands and feet were like blocks of ice.

The government and the Jewish Child and Family Service continued to help us until I was able to stand on my own two feet. The Canadian Jewish Congress (cjc) rented a basement apartment for us and provided us with some second-hand furniture, bedding, pots, pans, plates and other necessities. The apartment, which had a small bedroom and a fairly big kitchen, was in a bungalow near the Red River and a park. Andy slept in the kitchen on a cot, and I slept in the bedroom. The shower and toilet were in the furnace room.

The owners of the house were an elderly couple who had emigrated from the Soviet Union. The woman never learned to say my first name properly. Despite my frequent corrections, she always called me Iba instead of Ibi, which was the shortened form of my name used by everyone who knew me. Sometimes the man came through our kitchen to go to his apartment upstairs. I thought he was used to going that way and had just forgotten that the basement was now rented. He didn't even say hello as he walked through.

Another inconvenience stemmed from the work habits of the lady of the house. She slept through half the day and did her housework late at night. Several times I woke up from the sounds of her footsteps and her cleaning. One day, I tried to explain to her that I couldn't sleep because of her activities, which sometimes ran as late as three in the morning. She promised that she would write letters instead of cleaning. Despite the disturbances, I was very happy to be in my apartment. I was finally on my own.

My first shopping day in the nearby small supermarket was a difficult task. I could recognize things such as fruit, bread, chicken and milk, since it was obvious what they were, but the packages and tin cans puzzled me. I saw a tin can in the supermarket with what I thought was a picture of pancakes on it. The pancakes in the picture were covered with a liquid. Andy would be happy to have a few pancakes, I thought. So I bought the tin with the picture of the pancakes on it. When I opened it later at home, I was surprised to find tomato sauce, not pancakes!

I also needed some toothpicks at the supermarket. When I couldn't find them, I stopped a clerk and pointed to my teeth. He took me over to the counter where the toothbrushes were kept. I went back to the clerk, said no and repeated the gesture of pointing to my teeth. He then escorted me to the toothpastes. I gave up.

On another occasion, I bought a box of detergent with a picture of a floral printed towel on the side of the box. On opening the box at home, I found, to my surprise, that it did actually contain a light-blue, terry-cloth towel with blue flowers. I was delighted. After that, I always bought detergent with the same picture on the box, and after a while I had a nice collection of towels.

Although I had difficulties in adjusting to my new life in the first few months, I was in high spirits. Sometimes, when I think back on those days, I feel that I was happier than I was many years later, when I had my own bungalow. I'm not sure if I can explain why that was, but perhaps it had something to do with the circumstances I had left in Hungary, where I never had my own home and I was dependent on my in-laws.

In Winnipeg, there were a great many Ukrainian people. The women wore colourful printed wool kerchiefs and clothes in mixed, different colours, something that was a no-no for me. I thought that this was the Canadian way of dressing. Another thing I noticed was the behaviour of youths, which was different from that of youngsters in Hungary. On one occasion, an elderly man stepped onto a crowded bus. He was standing, supporting himself with his cane, when a woman, who was not young, stood up to offer him her seat. Two teenaged girls started to laugh when they saw this kind gesture. They had no idea that they should have offered their own seats. Andy jumped up from his seat whenever an older person boarded the bus. Finally he said to me, "Mother, I'm not sitting down even if there is a seat because I would just have to stand up again to give it to an older person." So he just stood during bus rides. Nowadays, however, Canadian youths are more polite to their elders than they were in those days.

Andy was enrolled at a school in Winnipeg in Grade 8, as he had been in Hungary. Unfortunately, after a couple of months, Andy was put back to Grade 6 because he did not know much English. He was heartbroken, and it took me a long time to reassure him that in a year he would catch up to his peers.

Andy's favourite teacher in Hungary sent him a letter in July of 1957, which helped him a lot.

I hope, my dear, that by the end of the year, you get used to the school and you make some friends. As I know your ability, I'm sure that you are going to be among the top students very soon. Among your old classmates, five of them have left the country with their parents. Those who stayed are studying diligently. You do the same to make your and your mother's life easier. I always think of you fondly as one of my best students.

When the Jewish community learned that I was a widow with a young child, they helped us even more. Sometimes, when I got home from work, I found a box at our doorstep full of warm clothes for Andy. On one occasion, a man who owned an electrical shop gave Andy a radio, and another man presented him with a record player and some records. All of these individuals were total strangers.

My first job was in a men's clothing factory. I was taken to the factory by a social worker, and I was hired as a sewing-machine operator. I had to learn so many things, including the language, at the same time. The sewing machines were monstrous, and learning to operate them was difficult. I had to sew trouser pockets, and after a short time I had to do them as piecework.

I earned twenty-six dollars a week, including overtime. To live on that salary for the two of us, I had to be very frugal. I used envelopes to keep my rent, grocery and spending money separate. I even managed to give Andy some allowance out of my paycheck. At that time, you could buy a week's worth of groceries for ten dollars.

Twice a week, I went to night school, where I made some Hungarian friends, and we got together on weekends and weekday evenings to study English. When my friends came to my apartment, one of us always had to hold one of the table legs so that the table would not collapse.

In the first few weeks in Winnipeg, Emil wanted to marry me; however, immigrants had to have been in the country for a certain amount of time in order to obtain a marriage licence. After a few months, Emil started to court a wealthy Jewish girl. Since he spoke Yiddish fluently, it wasn't difficult for them to communicate. They soon got married. I was glad that it had turned out this way, because he still disliked my son.

After about a year, Emil and his wife divorced. After the divorce, he came to see me again. I was surprised when he told me that he thought we could marry now, since Andy had grown and probably changed. I said, "My son hasn't changed, and please leave me alone. Even if I might have consented to marry you originally, I wouldn't do so after you left me for another woman." After awhile, Emil left the city.

In my eyes, Winnipeg looked like a big village. The small, colourful houses were like weekend cottages at Lake Balaton in Hungary. In contrast, the big department store called Hudson's Bay Company was impressive, and I enjoyed its huge selection of dresses, lingerie and just about everything else. Also, in the grocery stores, I could choose from a wide variety of foods.

One day after work, I went to buy groceries. There were many types of cheese, but I couldn't read the labels and didn't know which one to buy. I chose one at random. On the bus going home, I smelled an awful odour, as if someone hadn't washed his or her feet for weeks. I looked around in the bus but couldn't tell who the guilty one was. The odour accompanied me home, and only when I opened my grocery bag did I notice that the awful smell came from the cheese I had bought. I put it in the oven to mask the smell.

When the weather permitted, Andy and I would go for a stroll on our street. For every car we saw, Andy would tell me what make it was. I was fascinated by his knowledge about cars. One day, Andy asked me, "Mother, do you know when we are going to be rich?" "No, when?" I replied. "When we have soft drinks in our home every day and when I have a real bed and not this narrow cot on which I always bruise myself." I promised him that we were going to be that rich someday.

I wrote to my in-laws every month, and their first letter arrived on February 8, 1957. Their one-page airmail letter was written in such tiny letters that I had to strain my eyes to read it. Here is a section from that letter, which I still keep:

Our hearts are still very heavy, but we were glad to read that you are both all right. Your first letter was really interesting, and we showed it to everybody who asked about you and Andy. Mama and I hope that you both will have a secure and more peaceful life than here at home. The ruins are all cleaned up, and the city is starting to look like before the revolution. The electricity is restored, and the movies and shows in theatres are playing again.

I have some questions. Which way did you go and with whom? How long did the journey last? When did you reach the border? I hope neither of you were cold because here it was very cold at that time. Did you have enough money? Here everybody says that Canada is a good country and everybody could make a living there if they have work. I know that for all your life you were a diligent worker, and I'm sure you will do your best to provide all the necessities for you and Andy. Please write every tiny detail about your life, your health, your work and learning the new language. What do you do in your spare time? Do you have any friends?

Our home is so quiet and empty without you and Andy. The only joy we have is when you write to us. Imagine that my little budgie, Pityu, asks all the time, "Where is Ibi and Andy?"

~

After a few months, I was transferred to another factory, one making women's clothing. On one occasion, I was sewing a black skirt with red lining, and I sewed all of it with the wrong colour of thread. One of the workers noticed my mistake, but she maliciously waited until I had finished my work and then went to the forewoman and told her about my error. I had to take the entire skirt apart and do it over again with the right thread.

In the factory, a machine sold bottled soft drinks for ten cents each. One day, I saw empty bottles all over the place and, believing that the cleaning staff would just throw them in the garbage can, I collected them and took them home. Andy redeemed the empty bottles at the grocery store for two cents apiece. The next morning, I felt terribly embarrassed when the forewoman came over and told me that I was not supposed to take the bottles home because the owner reused them in the machine.

Andy also encountered difficulties, but his were in school. He had yet to make any friends, and he was very homesick. One afternoon when I arrived home, Andy was sitting on a chair bending down, pretending that he was busy with his shoelaces. When he didn't look up upon my greeting him, I asked, "What are you hiding, Andy?"

Then he looked at me, and I saw black and bloody bruises all over his face. "Oh, my God!" I gasped. "What happened to you?" Andy told me that he had had a fight with a boy who had called him "stinky Jew."

"Oh, no! Not again! Not here!" I cried out, hugging him and kissing his bruised face.

"But, Mother," he said, "you should see what I did to him! His bruises are worse than mine. And the teacher was on my side because I just reacted to the boy's remark." I washed Andy's face and tried to reassure him and myself that it had been only an isolated incident.

One night when we arrived home, Andy turned on the small radio. Suddenly, the whole apartment was filled with the beautiful music of the famous composer Johann Strauss II. Andy cried out, "Mother! Mother, do you hear it? A Hungarian song!" He laughed and cried with joy. My heart went out to him. "Darling," I said, "if you want to go back to your grandparents and friends, I will let you go. But I wouldn't go back for anything."

"Then I will not go either," he answered.

In the early summer of 1958, we moved to another apartment. This time we had our own tiny bathroom in the apartment, so we didn't have to worry anymore that somebody would walk into the furnace room while Andy or I were taking a shower. Our little home was now completely self-contained.

Andy still slept in the kitchen on the same cot, but in the corner of the kitchen was a kitchenette with a fridge and a stove. We used the kitchen, which was the biggest room, for everything. It served as the living room, dining room and study. Although the furniture consisted of the same second-hand pieces as before, I made the small apartment as cozy and pretty as I could. I hung white lace curtains in the windows and put a lovely printed tablecloth on the table and some inexpensive but colourful pictures on the walls. Every morning before work, I tidied my apartment and paused in the doorway to admire it before leaving.

One evening, Andy and I went to our first movie in Canada, *The Ten Commandments*, which made a big impression on both of us. When we came out of the cinema, everything looked so beautiful! It was early in January, and the Christmas lights and decorations were still up. We stopped at the first corner, and I looked around at the quiet street covered with thick, freshly fallen snow and the small coloured Christmas lights around the windows of the houses and on the trees and bushes. It was so peaceful and relaxing. I hugged my son and planted a kiss on his cheek.

"Are you all right, Mother?" he asked me.

"Yes, my son, I am." How could he understand my feeling of being free of every bad thing from my past?

Across from our apartment on the same floor was a Hungarian couple. They were about ten years younger than me, but despite the age difference, we became good friends. The woman, Ady, also worked in a clothing factory, and her husband, Eugene, worked in a bakery. Eugene had a positive influence on Andy, teaching him by example. Eugene worked during the night, and after sleeping until about two o'clock in the afternoon, he did some cooking or other work around the home. Eugene became like a big brother to Andy.

In Winnipeg, the weather was very unpredictable. One nice spring day in mid-May, I went to work dressed lightly. When I came out of the factory late in the afternoon, there was a snowstorm!

During our first summer in Canada, the CJC paid for Andy to go to a camp for the entire summer. The camp, near Kenora, Ontario, was on an island in Lake of the Woods. We received a list of clothes for him to take to the camp. After Andy had finished reading the list to me, he said, "Mother, I'm puzzled about one thing."

"What is that?" I asked him.

"I don't know why I would need rubber pyjamas."

I started to laugh because I knew it was a misunderstanding connected to a Hungarian word. On the list of items needed were cotton pyjamas. In Hungarian, "Cotton" was a brand name for condoms. Andy knew that a condom was made from rubber, and seeing the words "cotton pyjamas," he thought they also must be made of rubber. After I explained his misunderstanding, he also had a good laugh.

Andy had a very nice time at the camp. He had always had a charming way with females, which won him many admirers. Also, after half a year in Canada, he knew enough English to communicate with the other children.

A couple who also had a child in the camp took me to visit Andy one Sunday. The woman picked me up at my home and drove me to their beautiful house early in the morning. In their marvellous white kitchen, she prepared a lot of sandwiches and other food to take with us. We went by car, my first ride ever in an automobile, and I enjoyed the beautiful countryside and good weather.

Andy was so happy to see me. He showed me his cabin and his new friends, and he happily told me that he was able to swim in the lake, swimming for the first time since we had left Hungary.

∼

Andy worked after school as a delivery boy for a drugstore. He delivered items to customers by bicycle for fifty cents an hour. During the summer of 1958, he worked as a warehouse packer and earned forty-two dollars a week, which he gave to me for the household. I gave him back some of the money as allowance, which he saved to buy a camera. Andy enjoyed taking photos, just as his father had. When he had saved enough money, Andy bought a camera for twenty-eight dollars, which was more than I earned in a week.

Because I was a widow, all of my friends were looking for a husband for me. An elderly classmate of mine at night school talked about a man who was well off and wanted to get married. When I asked her how old this gentleman was, she said that he was forty-five, the right age for me. I agreed to meet him. He phoned me first, and that night he came to pick me up in his car. My first impression was that he looked much older than forty-five.

We went to a coffee shop, but before we went in, he gave me a ten-cent chocolate bar for my son. He talked about his business – he owned a delicatessen – and how busy he was. He was so busy that he hadn't had a vacation for fifteen years. I didn't really like him. Then I asked him (I didn't know it was impolite) how old he was, and he admitted to being sixty-five, a twenty-five-year difference between us. In addition, we couldn't communicate properly because of our language difference. I never went on another date with him. When my classmate wanted to introduce me to someone else, I thanked her and told her that I wasn't interested.

New Beginnings

In the late summer of 1958, we decided to move to Toronto. Andy found out that he had two classmates there from Hungary, and my sister Aranka and her family had moved there from Hamilton, where they had originally settled after leaving Hungary on December 24, 1956.

Aranka's husband, Jenö, had had a position in the Ministry of Agriculture in Budapest and had been a member of the Communist Party. However, he was very outspoken and had criticized the Party, despite his friends' warning. Consequently, he had been expelled from the Party and was subsequently accused of being an enemy of the regime. Jenö had felt that he and his family were in danger, so they too had decided to escape. Like us, they travelled via Austria, ending up in Vienna for several weeks, after which they went by ship to Halifax, arriving in the first week of March 1957.

During the thorough medical examinations, unfortunately, an X-ray showed a spot on Aranka's lung. She and Jenö were transferred to a sanatorium in Hamilton, where Jenö got a job as a cleaner. They stayed there for six months. During this time, frequent X-rays showed that the spot had neither grown nor moved, so Aranka had probably had it from birth. The doctors released her. I eventually learned of their whereabouts in Canada from a letter Mama sent from Hungary.

We decided to fly to Toronto at the end of August so Andy could start school in September. I told my plans to my boss, who was very understanding. He wrote me a letter of recommendation and even invited us for a Sabbath supper on the last Friday night before our departure. He and his wife presented us with a lovely gift of two silver candlesticks. I thanked them and promised to light the Sabbath candles every Friday night. Until that moment, I hadn't done this. My colleagues gave me a leather carry-on as a going-away present. Never before had I received any presents from my workplace.

In Toronto, we stayed the night with Aranka and her family. The next day, Andy and I went apartment hunting. I needed Andy for two reasons: he spoke English more fluently than I did, and he had a good sense of direction, unlike me. He always used to tell me, "Mother, if you want to go somewhere, always turn in the opposite direction you originally thought to go."

We started out in the morning around Kensington Market because I was told that rent was more reasonable there. We saw many "Flat to Let" signs in windows, but by early afternoon we still had had no luck. The landlords refused to rent to us either because they didn't want a teenager or because I didn't yet have a job.

Eventually, we found and rented a flat near Aranka's place on Cumberland Avenue. It contained two small furnished rooms and a kitchen. We had to share the bathroom with the owner and his family. Again, we had no privacy because we couldn't lock our door from the outside. There was only a latch inside.

My brother-in-law, Jenö, helped me get a job as a cleaning lady at Toronto Western Hospital, where he worked as an orderly. Although he had a doctorate in economics, he knew very little English, so he was glad to have any job.

I had been told that we might get some help from the welfare department for our new beginning, so Andy and I went there to make inquiries. There, we met a couple who had come from Vancouver and were also Hungarian. When the woman, Mary, learned that I was a widow, she asked if I would consider remarrying. I said that I would if

I could find a suitable man. "I know just the right man for you," Mary told me. "He was a comrade of my husband's in the labour camp in Hungary. He is forty-six years old and very hard-working. He is honest, clean and handsome, but he is from a small village in Hungary, so he is not a city person like you." I was interested, and Mary gave me her phone number to call her when I had a chance.

Andy enrolled in Central Technical School on Harbord Street. Some of his old schoolmates from Budapest were there, and he made some new friends as well. He was much happier than he had been at school in Winnipeg.

The next week, I started my new job at the hospital. I got a uniform – a blue dress – and I washed floors and toilets. After a while, I was promoted, and my new uniform was light brown with a green hem and collar and a half apron with green edging. I wasn't washing floors any more; instead, I was cleaning the patients' rooms and their toilets. I did this work for two years. During that time, I studied English, hoping that someday I would get a better job for myself.

One night, while cleaning out my purse, I found the phone number of my new friend, Mary, and called her. I told her I was working in a hospital and reminded her of her offer to fix me up with a suitable gentleman. Mary replied that she had mentioned me to exactly such a man, and he wanted to meet me very much. We set up a date for me to meet the man at the apartment of her friends Ica and Tibi for the following Sunday afternoon. I was curious about both the looks and the character of the man I was about to meet.

I dressed carefully in my best outfit, which I had received in Winnipeg as a handout. It was a black suit with a white blouse. They were in good condition and fit me perfectly. I fixed my thick, dark hair and put some lipstick on. I never used any other makeup. When I arrived at the given address, my date, another Emil, was already there, sitting in the living room with Mary and her husband. The first thing I noticed about him was his dark, wavy hair, which reminded me of my first husband. His round, smooth face suggested a much younger person than forty-six. He was neatly dressed in a dark grey suit, white shirt and grey-striped necktie. When he stood up as Mary introduced him, I also noticed that his height was about the same as my late husband's. I felt that he was as attracted to me as I was to him.

Ica served coffee and cake, and we talked about our lives in Canada. I was wearing a pair of knee-high nylons, and I remember pulling my skirt down a few times to cover my knees as I sat across from my date. Emil walked me home and told me he would call, which he did, the very next day. We dated mostly on weekends. He told me that he was lonely and homesick in Canada and was thinking of going back to Hungary. He also told me that he had been introduced to other women but hadn't liked them. "How about me?" I asked. "Do you like me, even with a sixteen-year-old son?"

"Yes, I like you. Otherwise, I wouldn't have called you after our first date," Emil replied.

We dated for about three months before we made plans to marry. I talked over my plans with my son, who was very happy for me. He realized how hard it was for me to be alone. Andy understood that I had been burdened by the responsibility of trying to be both mother and father to him. I told Andy that I thought that my future husband was a wonderful man but that he was from a small village and therefore might have different interests from us. I asked my son to always treat his stepfather with respect.

Emil had a very good friend, Joe, who had arrived in Toronto with his wife, Edith, many years earlier and who had sent Emil's airplane ticket to him in Austria when Emil had written that he was there waiting for his turn to come to Canada. Emil took me to Joe and Edith's home to introduce me and, I thought, to ask their opinion of me. Joe told him to marry me before I changed my mind.

Our wedding, which Joe and Edith organized, took place on December 14, 1958. We had a buffet-style reception with plenty of food. There were about fifty people, most of them from Emil's side, because I had only Aranka and her family on my side. On Sunday, my wedding day, the ceremony was scheduled for two in the afternoon. In the morning, I went to a Hungarian hairdresser nearby. Quite a few ladies were ahead of me. I didn't know any of them, but most of them knew my future husband from back home. One of the women said to the hairdresser, "Make a nice hairdo, Elizabeth, please, because today I'm invited to a wedding."

"Whose wedding are you invited to?" asked Elizabeth.

"I know only the groom, Emil Grossman, but I don't know the bride," was the answer.

Overhearing the discussion, I smiled to myself and said loudly, "Please, Elizabeth, make a nice hairdo for me, too, because I'm the bride of Emil Grossman."

Everyone laughed.

At my wedding, I wore a royal-blue suit, a white silk blouse and a white velvet hat with a short veil, which covered half of my face. My fiancé gave me a bouquet of pale yellow flowers. Carrying the bouquet, I slowly walked up to the canopy alone. Emil was there, surrounded by his best friends, with the rabbi across from him waiting for my arrival.

The ceremony was short but lovely. The rabbi, who was also Hungarian, gave a speech about two lonely people in a foreign country who had found each other. He wished us all the best and asked us to keep the Jewish faith and observe the Jewish traditions. Andy walked around with a camera taking pictures. We didn't have a professional photographer, but Andy's photos turned out very well.

We had already rented an apartment at the corner of Markham and College Streets. It had two bedrooms and another small room, which we later rented to a young Hungarian man. We also had a kitchen, living room and bathroom. Finally, Andy had his own room and a comfortable new bed. And, oh wonder of wonders, the week after we moved in Emil bought a television!

I still worked in the hospital, but I hated my work there. I started my job at six in the morning, which meant that I had to get up a little before five. Also, I felt that I was capable of more than cleaning washrooms. The factory where Emil worked as a cabinetmaker was far from our apartment, and every morning he got a ride with Hungarian friends. We started to talk about buying a used car. This would have been a luxury in Hungary, and we had never been able to buy one there, but in Canada it was more of a necessity. When we decided it was time to buy a car, after much looking and bargaining, we finally bought a two-year-old Chevrolet. It was silvery blue with dark blue seats. It was a beauty, and it was ours!

I felt very rich owning a car. All of our friends came to inspect our new purchase. Emil took a few lessons and soon learned to drive. I remembered how surprised I had been when I saw a cleaning lady driving to work in her own car in Winnipeg. "Look, Andy," I had said to my son. "Here in Canada, even the cleaning ladies own a car." Now that we had ours, I understood its importance.

Emil and I hired a sixteen-year-old Canadian student to teach us English one night a week. Sometimes, instead of teaching us the language or its grammar, he taught us Canadian ways, such as how to make cheeseburgers in our oven. During this time, I still attended English classes at night school, and it finally paid off in April of 1961. We had been reading an English newspaper every day to keep up to date with the news. One day, I saw an advertisement for various jobs at the Bank of Montreal. I gathered all my courage and went to apply for a clerical job.

At that time, there was an age limit for hiring staff, and at forty-five I was over the limit. For this reason, they didn't want to hire me, but I was desperate to get out of my cleaning work at the hospital. I started to cry. Then I remembered something I had read the previous evening. Still crying, I said, "You don't want to hire me because my name is Grossman and I'm a Jew! Just last night, I read in the paper that the banks don't want to hire Jews because they think that after a while the Jews will want to own the banks."

When I had first read this, I thought I hadn't understood it correctly. But the story was true, and the management wanted to prove that it was not. "We already have Hebrew girls," said the person in charge, who then hired me to further prove the point. My job was in the coupons and bonds department, and I didn't have to start work until nine o'clock in the morning!

~

My sister Elizabeth and her family had immigrated legally to Israel in the summer of 1957. In her first letter to me, she wrote that she and her family were bitterly sorry to have made that move because life was difficult and they were having trouble making ends meet. When, in her next letter, Elizabeth wrote that a stray cat had eaten her much-treasured chicken and that she had been crying all day long, I decided to send her and her family a parcel. I put together a package that contained instant coffee, sugar, bittersweet chocolates, canned food, coffee beans and even toys for Tomi, Elizabeth and Frank's son.

Elizabeth wrote that they were incredibly grateful to receive the goodies and that I should have seen Tomi's joy at getting all those toys and chocolates. Tomi also wrote a whole page in his mother's letter thanking me for his presents and telling us that he already spoke a little Hebrew. It was a nice letter from a not quite ten-year-old boy.

Even after living there for a few years, Elizabeth still sounded disconsolate in her letters. In one, she asked us if we could bring her and her family to Canada. She wrote that if we could lend them the money, they would pay us back later. After my husband read the letter, I asked him, "What do you think about their problem? Would it be possible to help them?"

"Of course we'll help them. She is your sister." I kissed him for his generosity. We started to work on the arrangements and soon sent Elizabeth three plane tickets.

Elizabeth and her family arrived on a sunny summer day in 1960. We were just about to go to the airport to pick them up when, looking out the window, I saw a limousine with them in it pull up to the front of our building. They had decided to take an earlier flight and surprise us with their arrival. As they got out of the limo taxi, I noticed that my nephew, Tomi, had changed a lot. He had been eight years old when I had last seen him, and now he was a much taller twelve-year-old. I ran down the steps to greet them, calling out loudly to Emil, "They are here already!"

After greeting them warmly, Emil helped take their suitcases up to their room, which had been our tenant's before we sent him away to make room for my sister and her family. We helped Elizabeth's husband, Frank, secure a job in a textile factory as a cutter, and Elizabeth took over my old cleaning job for a short time. We found an inexpensive apartment for them, and after three weeks they moved out on their own. Tomi had no difficulty in school. He picked up English quickly and was an excellent student. He eventually became a civil engineer. We introduced Elizabeth and her family to our friends, and on weekends we took them to beaches and on other excursions.

Meanwhile, the big day for us to become Canadian citizens finally arrived. On May 10, 1962, my husband, son and I became Canadians. I was so happy! I had my family, my home, my work and my health in my new adopted country. Did I need anything more?

Visits and Journeys

My former in-laws' letters from Hungary arrived every month, and I answered them right away. Every year, on Mother's Day, Zolti's mother sent flowers to me through a Hungarian flower shop in Toronto. When I had written to my in-laws about my marriage to Emil, they were happy for me. In his letters, Papa started to hint at how much he and Mama would like to see us and to get to know my new husband. I approached Emil and asked if he would agree to bring them over for a visit. He said yes without any hesitation.

In my next letter to Budapest, I wrote that Emil and I would start the necessary steps to bring them to Canada for a visit. Their answer to my letter was so moving that Emil had to turn aside to wipe away his tears. Papa wrote:

You are the most generous two people in the world. First you, my daughter, who always kept in contact with us, unlike many others who left their parents behind and very seldom or never wrote to them. And now your husband, who has never known us, agreed to our coming over. We will appreciate this forever! We are the happiest couple in the whole city to know we will soon see our only grandson, the light of our eyes, and you, and to know our new son. Because Emil is going to be our son, instead of our own whom we lost so young.

Mama and Papa had already applied to the Hungarian government for a permit to come to Canada. We took time off work to go to the immigration office for their visas.

"What relationship are these people to you?" asked the officer in charge.

"They are my late husband's parents," I told him.

"But you are married now. Is your present husband offering to bring over your first in-laws?" he asked.

"Yes, he agrees," I said.

Looking surprised, the clerk said, "Your husband must be a very good human being."

After we got the documents we needed, we sent two airplane tickets to Mama and Papa. It was a cold, sunny spring day in March 1963 when we all went to the airport to meet my in-laws, whom Andy and I hadn't seen for six long years. Our excitement grew when we heard that their airplane had arrived. Finally they were in front of us: Papa, still tall and slim in his early seventies, and Mama, small and much rounder than I remembered her.

Mama's first words to Andy were, "Light of my eyes, you are not a little boy any more; you are a fine young man." It was true. Andy was now a very handsome twenty-year-old. After many hugs and kisses and some tears, we drove Mama and Papa home to our two-bedroom apartment on Clovelly Avenue, south of Eglinton and west of Oakwood. They were impressed with our 1958 silver-blue Chevrolet, which was still in good condition, and they were equally impressed by our apartment, which was on the top floor of a triplex. I gave them Andy's bedroom, and Andy moved to the living-room couch. When Mama took off her coats, she slimmed down instantly. She had worn three coats, and two of them were a couple of their many presents. One coat was for Andy, and one was for me.

Since Andy, Emil and I had to go to work, my in-laws were on their own during the day. Mama did the cooking despite my protests, but she said that she had to have something to do. She even asked if Emil had any socks with holes in them that she could mend. I said laughingly that in Canada we didn't mend socks if they were worn out; we bought another pair. Mama just loved to answer the telephone. She didn't have one at her home in Budapest. One night our telephone rang, and Mama hurried to answer it. "May I talk to Andy?" a young girl asked in Hungarian. "He can't come right now, my sweet child, because my grandson is in the bathtub washing his tuchis," she answered. She meant his behind.

My in-laws took long walks hand-in-hand in the neighbourhood. One day, they even walked along Bathurst and stepped into Holy Blossom Temple, a reform synagogue; they were surprised that men did not have to wear *yarmulkes*, skullcaps, inside.

On weekends, we took excursions together to the beach, to High Park, to Edwards Gardens and to other destinations. When Emil and I had some vacation time, Emil drove us to Montreal, where my in-laws had old friends to visit.

One early morning in late spring, we all went to a farm in the Niagara region, where we had friends. After lunch, a young girl came over from the nearby dairy farm where she lived with her family. Emil happened to know her family from Hungary. He introduced the girl, Magdi, to us, and Andy talked and joked with her. Magdi asked if we would like to meet her parents and take a tour of her family's farm. We went over for a short visit and had a lovely time.

One day in May, when I arrived home and stepped into the living room, I was greeted by the sweet fragrance of my favourite flowers, lilacs. There was a huge bouquet of them in the centre of the table.

"Mama, where did you get the flowers?" I asked her.

"As Papa and I were strolling along the sidewalk, I saw a lady tending her garden," she said. "There was a beautiful bush with very dark lilacs on it. I know lilac is your favourite, so I wanted to have some for you."

"But how did you ask for them, Mama? I know that you don't know any English," I said.

"It was easy," she answered. "I stopped, pointed to the tree and put my two palms together as if I were praying. The lady understood what I wanted and cut a bunch of the flowers for me."

"How did you thank her?"

"Oh, I just blew a kiss and smiled at her, and she smiled back at me."

My in-laws' most memorable outing was a day trip to Niagara Falls. All Hungarians back in Hungary had heard about these falls. We even had a song that praised this wonder of nature, but we had never imagined just how beautiful the falls were until we saw them. The falls had the same effect on Mama and Papa as they had had on us when we first saw them. We had an unforgettable day together.

With my in-laws' fiftieth wedding anniversary approaching, we decided to celebrate with a surprise party for them. We planned the party for a Sunday in July. I prepared the food and ordered a chocolate cake with the message "Happy 50th Wedding Anniversary" written in frosting on top. I also ordered a magnificent floral centrepiece composed of two low flowerpots on either side of a tall one. Gold dust was sprinkled over the red roses in each of the pots. Three gold-coloured candles were in the middle of each pot. We hid the centrepiece in the garage.

My sister Aranka and her husband, Jenö, lived walking distance away from us, and I told them that I would send my in-laws over to them on that Sunday afternoon so I could set the table in our home. When I told my in-laws to walk over to my sister's home, Mama asked me, "Why do you want to get rid of us today?"

"I don't, Mama. Aranka told me she wanted to have you over for an espresso." My in-laws walked over to Aranka's. At about five-thirty, my family started to arrive. Elizabeth with her husband, Frank, and son, Tomi, came, as did Aranka's daughter, Marianna, with her husband, Laci. Finally, Aranka and Jenö arrived with Mama and Papa. It was a family get-together, which we seldom had had before. Everyone brought presents, cards and flowers.

After supper, when my in-laws started to open their packages, tears of joy ran down their cheeks. Mama immediately changed into the light-grey silk dress that Emil and I had bought for her. That day was another memorable one among many with my in-laws during their visit.

All too soon, our visit came to an end. Our farewell was almost as emotional as the welcome had been when they had first arrived. They needed an extra suitcase to take home all the presents they had received. We escorted them to the airport and promised that we would come to Hungary to visit them. After my in-laws left, we went back to our old routines, but we talked about that visit for a long time.

~

My first trip outside Canada with my husband was to Israel. Until then, we had gone on smaller trips to Montreal, Ottawa and the United States. But in 1965, we made plans to go to Israel and to visit Paris for a few days on our way back. While I had lived in Hungary, I had never had the chance or the money to see other countries. I was excited to see Israel, where my husband's only brother and his family lived.

When I first walked on the streets in Israel – a place I had wanted to go to with my little boy in 1949 when we were captured – I had the feeling that I was really home, because it felt as though in Israel, no one would hurt me for being Jewish. My brother-in-law laughed when, pointing to a street sweeper, I asked him, "Is he Jewish also?"

Alex and Emil were overjoyed to see each other after many long years. This was the first time that I had met my brother-in-law, his wife, Sarah, and their eight-year-old son, Avram. Alex had escaped from Hungary in 1949 and had gone to Israel the same year. Life there was very hard back then. He settled down in a small *moshav* and lived in a tent. He wanted to start farming, but to do so, he had to be married, so he married the first available woman he met. After the marriage, the government supplied them with seeds for grass, a cow and materials for a small house, which they had to build themselves.

Alex and Sarah were well off by the time we arrived, and Alex wanted to pay all our expenses in the country. He bought me a topaz ring in an eighteen-carat gold setting, which I treasure and have worn ever since.

The village in which they lived had a total population of roughly two hundred people, all of whom were Hungarian. Alex introduced us to all his neighbours. On one of our visits to a neighbour's home, upon hearing my name, the host asked, "Are you the one whose fiancé was Béla Boros?"

"Yes, I am. What do you know about him?" I asked.

"I was Béla's and Zolti's comrade in the concentration camp," he said.

When he mentioned my late husband's name, I had a hard time not showing how emotional it made me. Then he suddenly asked me, "Would you like to see Béla?" I looked at my husband, who nodded. "Yes," I said.

It was a very unusual situation the next day when my present husband took me over to the man's house in a horse carriage to meet my former fiancé. Béla looked a bit older, and his thick, wavy hair needed a cut. Around his big blue eyes were new tiny wrinkles when he smiled. We hugged each other, and his first question was, "How is little Andy?" Then he wanted to see pictures of Andy, which I showed him. Béla never remarried. I felt sorry for him because he looked so lonely, but circumstances and fate had pulled us apart.

That was the last time that I ever saw Béla. Some years later, another comrade of my first husband's, who also had lived in Israel since 1949 with his family, wrote to me about Béla. Béla had visited them frequently and he adored their children. He had been on his way to see them, with a couple of chocolate bars in his shirt pocket for the children, when he suffered a heart attack. Béla was fifty years old when he died.

~

For more than ten years, the thought of going back to Hungary made me very uncomfortable. In my first few years in Canada, I had recurring nightmares in which I returned to Hungary and then was not allowed back into Canada. I would wake up perspiring and sometimes in tears, relieved that it had been only a dream. But after my in-laws' repeated requests – about a dozen – I decided to go back to see them. In the summer of 1968, both Emil and I travelled to Budapest.

Arriving on a warm summer day, we took a taxi to 16 Népszinház utca. That was the apartment building where I had lived for a few years with my Zolti and, after his death, with his parents. That was the place to which I had brought home our new baby. That was the home where I had slept fully dressed during the night, in case the police came for us, and the home from which we had been taken away, Zolti to a labour camp, Andy and I to a ghetto. It was the home to which I hurried back in the hour of our liberation to beg some food for Papa, who was dying from hunger. From this home, I had escaped in 1949, only to be captured, and had escaped again, with success, in November 1956.

In 1968, I stood in the yard of that very building, looking around before I entered the kitchen of our apartment. Weeds grew between the red stones in the courtyard, and the whole building was kept from collapsing by many huge beams.

As I stepped into the kitchen, with Emil behind me, I saw Mama at the stove cooking supper for us. Hearing the door open, she looked up, cried, "You are here!" and ran to us with outstretched arms. We held each other, weeping. Papa came out of his room. He, too, hugged and kissed us, and tears welled up behind his eyeglasses. Seeing his long, white hair, the tears in his eyes and his much heavier body, caused by his liver ailment, memories rushed again into my mind. Was he the same man who once, a long time ago, had wanted to report me to the authorities for my escape from the country? Now I felt sorrow and love toward him. I wanted to be with him and Mama as much as I could during the brief three weeks we were in Hungary.

The first few days, neighbours from the building who knew me came to see us. Mama proudly introduced Emil with "He is Ibi's husband, my Emil." She loved him very much. During our visit to Hungary, we also went to Emil's hometown. When we arrived in this small village, where everyone knew him and his family, he was welcomed as if he were a brother to everyone. We stayed a couple of days at his old neighbour's house. In every home we visited, we were offered a glass of wine. I didn't want to be impolite, so I sipped a little wine at everyone's place. Of course, I was happy and laughing from all this, and people told Emil how nice and merry his wife was. In my entire life, I haven't drunk as much wine as in those two days.

We also went to Lake Balaton with my cousin Joe Fabian, who had a cottage there. Joe, who was from my mother's side of the family, had lost his family in the Holocaust and had remarried and had two children after the war. Our three weeks flew by, and then we had to return to Toronto for our work.

It was always harder for those who stay behind. Seeing Mama and Papa standing at the front of their building, waving goodbye as we left for the airport in a taxi, was very sad. I promised to visit them again soon.

The Circle of Life

Andy worked at Toronto City Hall as a draftsman and often went to the bank in the building. Coincidentally, one of the tellers was Magdi, the girl we had met five years earlier when visiting the dairy farm with my in-laws. Andy and Magdi dated for a while, and one day in the early fall of 1968 Andy announced that he had proposed to Magdi. The next Sunday, we all went to Magdi's parents' place to celebrate the engagement. Both sides were satisfied with their children's choice. The wedding took place on December 15, 1968, in Hamilton, one day after Emil's and my tenth wedding anniversary.

Magdi, a lovely, family-oriented girl, clearly loved her parents and only sister, Margaret. She also seemed to be happy to have another father and mother, as she called Emil and me after the wedding. Magdi and I had a good relationship, more like mother and daughter than mother and daughter-in-law.

Two years after they got married, Magdi became pregnant. On a gorgeous day, Sunday, May 23, 1971, we were invited to our friends' home for a barbecue. Since Magdi was expecting her baby any day, I told Andy where to reach us just in case. We had just started to eat when the phone rang. Somehow I knew it was good news. When my friend passed me the phone, I heard my son's voice on the other end. "Hello, Mother. Congratulations! You have just become a grandmother."

I was thrilled and excitedly asked him many questions, not waiting for any answers. I was overjoyed to have my first grandchild but a little bit confused, too. Was I an old lady now, I wondered? When I was a child, all the grandmothers were old and white-haired.

The baby, named David, was a perfect little thing. After the first three months, he spent many weekends with us. A good-natured baby, David was very easy to care for. In his first years, he was tiny for his age but very advanced in other ways. At ten months he had already started to walk, and a month later he said his first words.

In that year, 1971, a sad event also occurred. My sister's husband, Jenö, who was sixty-two years old, died suddenly of a heart attack. My husband and I were in New York visiting Emil's sick cousin when it happened; Andy called to tell us the news, and said that the funeral would take place the following day.

The next day, when we arrived home, we had just enough time to get to the funeral. Aranka was devastated by the loss of her husband. As the years passed, she became more and more bitter and lonely. I understood her feelings and sympathized with her because I had gone through the same loneliness. But she said that my situation had been different, because I had been young and still had some hope for the future. She was right.

~

I continued to write letters diligently to my in-laws every month, and Papa always answered. His writing was even and small, like tiny pearls. When he became sick, it showed in his letters: the writing started to appear much larger and uneven.

One day early in 1973, we received a letter from Mama's nephew Jenö. He wrote that Mama's remaining nephews and nieces wanted to celebrate their aunt and uncle's sixtieth wedding anniversary. Mama had had eleven sisters and brothers, but only three of them survived the Holocaust. However, she had quite a few nephews and nieces. Jenö also wrote that Papa was very sick with terminal cancer and did not want this celebration. Nevertheless, the relatives had decided to go ahead with their plans, and they invited us to the anniversary party.

Emil and I decided to go to Hungary to see them. This time, it was a very sad meeting. Papa was in bed the whole time, too weak to get up. I sat at his bedside holding his hand or stroking his face. He smiled at me and said in a low voice, "You are a good woman. You always have been good to us. God bless you."

Emil and I, along with Mama and Papa's other relatives, were at Papa's bedside when the rabbi remarried them on their sixtieth wedding anniversary. We made a toast to Papa's good health, and he took a little of his wedding cake from my hand. I was glad to have been there that summer, because a couple of months later, Papa passed away.

After his death, Mama took in her nephew Jenö and his wife, Irma. Jenö and Irma didn't have their own apartment, and by taking them into hers, Mama was ensuring that her apartment would automatically go to them after her death.

Mama had trouble coping with the departure of her husband of sixty years. When she also became sick, Irma took good care of her.

Then, one day, we received a letter from Irma saying that if we wanted to see Mama alive, we had better travel to Hungary soon. It was Christmas 1974. This time, I travelled with my son. When Mama saw her only grandchild after so many years, she wept and told him repeatedly, "You are here, light of my eyes. You are here." During the two weeks' visit, I stayed with Mama most of the time, but she sent Andy out to enjoy the city. When Andy and I took her outside for a short walk, she was so weak we had to support her on both sides.

A few months after we returned home, I received a telegram from Budapest, and my heart started to beat loudly. The news in it couldn't be about anyone but Mama. Opening it, I saw these few words: "Your mother-in-law died peacefully yesterday. Irma." I sat down with the telegram, and my thoughts went far back in time. I had married her only son when I was very young, and she had been like a second mother to me.

Mama was the one who had taken me to the hospital when my child was about to be born. When I had had to say goodbye to my Zolti, and we clung to each other, crying, Mama was the one who had gently separated us. She had tried to be strong for our sake. Later, when we had all been marched from our homes, it was Mama who had gone to a policeman whom she knew from her hometown to beg for my life. In the ghetto, Mama had almost starved to death because she insisted that Andy and I take the few small buns she made from the last grams of flour and water. When we learned the terrible news about my husband's death, Mama had comforted me, though her loss was also great. In 1949, when I decided to escape from Hungary with my child, only Mama had known about it and, holding back her tears, had escorted us to the train. After we had been caught and put in jail, she came to that strange city to take her grandson home.

The telegram said she was gone. A piece of my life was gone with her.

My Future

My grandson, David, was six years old when his mother told him that the next day she would know if she was having another baby. David could hardly wait for the next day. After his mother had informed him that he was going to have a baby brother or sister, he jumped on his bike and drove around the neighbourhood yelling, "I'm going to have a baby!"

One cold morning in February 1978, I got up earlier than usual. It was a Sunday, and I didn't have to go to work. Stepping into the kitchen, I saw a piece of white paper on the table. Curious, I picked it up. It was in my son's handwriting. *Here is Kati!! Born 3:10 a.m. today. She is eight and a half pounds. Her hair is black, her eyes blue, and she has chubby cheeks.* My son and daughter-in-law had kept the baby's arrival a secret until after the birth so as not to worry me.

I was sixty-two the year Kati was born, and that same year, I decided to take early retirement from the bank. The staff threw a very lovely party for me at the assistant manager's house. I was the centre of attention and felt like a bride at a bridal shower. I received a dozen crystal wineglasses from my colleagues.

On my last day at work, my colleagues sent me out of the office on some excuse. While I was gone, they put a bouquet of red roses, a cheque and a huge card on my desk. I was very moved and went to thank and hug every one of them. I managed to smile during my farewell, but as soon as I closed the office door behind me, I started to cry. Seventeen years is a very long time to work with a group of people, and I felt that I was saying goodbye to a part of my family.

During my first week at home, I dreamt I was in the bank looking for a job. A lot of women lined up in front of me. Finally I got a job, too, and I wanted to get into an elevator to go to the appointed floor, but I couldn't reach any of them no matter how fast I ran. At each elevator, the door closed before I could step in. Perhaps the dream meant that I was apprehensive not to be in the workforce any longer. However, I looked forward to the new adventures my future would bring.

I joined a seniors group that was close to our home, and I occupied myself with many activities, such as painting, needlework, crocheting and folk dancing. Tuesday nights I took a folk dancing class at Earl Bales Park; Thursday afternoons I went to the Baycrest Terrace retirement residence and read my stories in Hungarian to a small group of Hungarian residents. I had joined a creative writing group, and I also did some volunteer work at the Hospital for Sick Children.

The hospital playroom where I volunteered every Monday was bright and cheerful. The morning sun came through two huge windows. As soon as I entered the room, I would put the children's favourite record on the record player, take the toys out of the cupboard and spread them on the small tables. After I put the "Open" sign on the door at nine o'clock, the nurses started to bring the children in. Some of them were in wheelchairs or beds. By that time, my boss, a young woman, was usually on the ward visiting the children, checking to see whether they were allowed to come to the playroom.

Almost every week, I saw different faces. Only a few of the children stayed longer than one week. I worked in the orthopaedic surgery ward. Fortunately, the parents were allowed to stay with their children any time of the day. However, some children were from out of town or their parents were working, and they could see their parents only at night or on weekends.

Sometimes we had so many children in the playroom that I had to ask the nurses to take some of them back to their rooms because there were too many to handle. I knew I shouldn't show any of my feelings, but it was hard not to. One morning a new little girl was wheeled in, lying on her tummy in her crib. Her long, curly blond hair spread across her back, and her chubby hands clasped the sides of the crib. She was motionless, and when I stroked her hair, she startled at my unexpected touch. I spoke gently, patting her back. She was awake but didn't open her eyes. Soon her parents came with a beautiful bouquet of flowers and put it beside her head. When I stepped away to tend to another child, a nurse told me that the little girl with the cherubic face was blind. I went out to the corridor so that no one would see my tears. While there, I heard a baby crying, so I went to that room. A child of maybe six months was crying her heart out. There was a bottle beside her, but it was out of her reach. It was against regulations to pick up any baby, but I couldn't help but take the tiny thing out of her crib and cradle her in my arms. She stopped crying, only too happy to be picked up. She looked at me and smiled with tears still in the corners of her eyes. As I rocked her back and forth, she fell asleep, and I gently put her back in her crib. I returned to the playroom with both the baby's and my tears dried.

At twelve noon, we had to take the children back to their rooms for lunch. I would put away the toys, tidy up the room and close the door behind me. Out in the beautiful, sunny street, I tried to forget all the misery, but I couldn't stop thinking of it for a long while.

Bittersweet Budapest

While my in-laws were alive, I had felt an obligation to visit them. With them gone, I thought I would never go back to Hungary. In 1983, however, my grandson, David, expressed a desire to see the country from which his parents and grandparents had come. I thought of going back home with David.

Did I write "home"? My home is in Canada, the country that took us in, gave me work and a new life. I think maybe I still thought of Hungary as "home" because, despite what had happened there, it was the country where I was born and raised. As much as I wanted to forget that I was Hungarian, I couldn't, just as I couldn't forget our suffering and all the killing that had taken place in Hungary. In the ghetto, we were close to death so many times. I had only one goal then – to live! I never dreamt, then, that someday I would be able to go abroad and return with my grandson.

As David's twelfth birthday approached, Emil and I decided to take him to Hungary as a birthday present. He was ecstatic. However, I requested two things from him: First, he had to write a daily diary entry while in Hungary; second, he had to learn more of the Hungarian language. David already understood quite a lot of Hungarian, but he spoke only a few words. During the three months between his birthday and the end of the school year, when we would be leaving, David improved his Hungarian a great deal.

When the day came for our departure, David was very excited. This was his first trip outside his country of birth and also his first time on an airplane. It was a long journey.

I had written to my in-laws' niece Irma and her boyfriend (her husband had died some years before) to tell them that we would be visiting Hungary, and Irma offered her apartment, which she had inherited from my in-laws, the same apartment in which Andy and I had lived before our escape. I thanked Irma and accepted her offer, because I knew that the apartment was nice and cool during the hot summer.

As soon as we got off the plane at the Budapest airport around four o'clock in the afternoon, we went to a waiting room where I saw Irma, a tall woman, among the crowd. Although not related to us by blood, she was better to us than any close relative. She received us with open arms. David was so tired that when we got to Irma's apartment, he went to bed and slept through until the next day at noon.

We tried to take David to as many places as we could. For a few days, we visited the village where Emil had lived. For a city boy like David, everything was interesting and exciting in the small Hungarian village: the pigs in the pigpen, the pigeons on the roof and the chickens in the yard. Dogs and cats ran about freely. David was fascinated at how the cows knew their homes when they came back from pasture every afternoon.

In the family we stayed with, there were two girls – one was five and the other was nine. The nine-year-old, Vicki, showed David around. They fed the pigs and chickens together. Most of the children in the village wanted to see the young foreigner from Canada. With some of them, we exchanged small souvenirs. Once, while we were visiting a family in the village, the host said to David, "You are as lovely as a girl!" David, who understood the man's words, got angry and answered in Hungarian, "Get out!" pointing at the door. Everybody laughed and thought it was rather cute that David was sending the host out of his own home.

The family had a car, and they took us to a famous tourist attraction, a 6.4-kilometre-long stalactite cave in a town called Aggtelek. Light bulbs hanging from the ceiling of the cave provided just enough light for us to see where we were stepping. The stone formed different shapes, and icy water dripped down the walls. A guide led us through from the entrance to the exit at the other end.

Back in Budapest, we took David to the famous Hungarian circus and the zoo and, with an English-speaking guide, on sightseeing excursions around the city. We went to the outdoor swimming pool, Palatinus, where David's father, as a child, had rung the bell to signal the start of the artificial waves. We also went to the indoor swimming pool where Andy had been training for the Olympics before we escaped. I showed David his father's school and the nearby playground where Andy had played football with his friends.

I managed to get a ticket on a tour bus to go around Lake Balaton, which the local people called the "Hungarian Sea." The best fish came from there. The water is warm, and you can wade out for miles before it gets deep. Also, the whole region is famous for its grapes and wines. We ate lunch in a lovely restaurant where the tables were set in a garden full of geraniums and other flowers. Two Roma played the violin during our lunch, while we sipped wine from the Badacsonyi area, one of the best wine-growing regions in Hungary. The wine made me giddy and I laughed continuously, calling David by my son's name. David smilingly asked me, "Are you tipsy, Mama? I'm your grandson, David." He had to remind me a few more times of his name, but I didn't think that it was only the wine that caused my slip-up. It was the fact that David was almost the same age as Andy had been when we lived in Budapest before leaving the country.

On our way back to Budapest, our tour guide asked the passengers, who were from sixteen different countries, to each sing a song from their country. David was shy at first when the guide asked him to represent Canada with his song. Finally he did, and after he finished, he started to sing Hebrew songs as well. We were pleasantly surprised when some of the passengers joined him in the Hebrew songs.

During the summer in Budapest, the theatres and opera houses were closed, but there were a few outdoor theatres where musicals were performed. We were lucky to get tickets to a well-known Hungarian musical called *Wedding at Ecser*. David enjoyed it tremendously. We visited the charming Margaret Island, the picturesque Fisherman's Bastion and the gracefully built parliament buildings. We also took David to the 125-year-old synagogue, the Dohány, which was part of the ghetto in 1944. Now it is a tourist attraction. Services are still held in the old synagogue, and we attended a Saturday morning service.

On another outing, we went to a ceramics museum to see the works of a famous sculptor, Margit Kovács. The museum was in Szentendre, a small town on the bank of the Danube River, about a one-hour train ride from Budapest. The town, with its cobblestones, narrow streets and small houses, reminded me of my birthplace, Pécs. As I was walking in the unknown but still familiar streets, I forgot who and where I was. I was a little girl again, hopping from stone to stone, looking through the low windows of the little houses. On the next corner, if I turned right, or maybe left, I would step into Father's small tinsmith shop.

I stopped for a second to decide which way to turn when my grandson interrupted my thoughts. "Which way should we go, Mama?" he asked. Suddenly I came back from the past. I hugged my darling grandson and said, "Just straight ahead, életem." The Hungarian word *életem*, a term of endearment I used with David many times, means "my life."

Életem

The following year, another big event came up in our family. On the morning of Saturday, June 16, 1984, a handsome boy with greenish-blue eyes and light brown wavy hair stood on the pulpit of our synagogue. His cheeks were smooth and peach-coloured with excitement. David courageously and charmingly recited his part from the Torah, becoming a bar mitzvah. As I admired him, I couldn't believe that time had passed by so fast and that my baby grandson had become a man according to Jewish law. Tears of joy poured down my face as I listened to Andy's speech, especially when he said that David was a link in a chain that was nearly broken, and that he was living proof of the miracle of life, of Judaism and of tradition. How right Andy was. Because of sickness and hunger, my son's life had been a flickering flame in the wind. It was a miracle that he had lived. And now our family chain, which had almost been broken, would continue through David.

David's speech was also lovely. He thanked his parents, grandparents and relatives for their love and support. Of course, he mentioned his little sister, Kati, who was six years old at that time and gave him a lot of trouble when he babysat her. "But I love you anyway," he said. Mentioning us in his speech, David said, "Mama and Papa, I have spent much time with you since I was little and stayed at your home on many weekends. The little trips and adventures we have been on together, with your teaching me along the way a different perspective on life, have enabled me to appreciate the kind of life I have here." David looked at us and said, "I thank you." I am happy, *életem*, that you learned from us to value your life here, I answered him silently.

Book of Tears

I put down the little book I had received from the Jewish community of Pécs in 1987, and, covering my eyes with my hands, I cried and cried. The little twenty-by-fifteen-centimetre book had the title *Book of Tears* embossed in gold letters in Hungarian and Hebrew on the black cover and a black silk cord to keep the pages together. On every page, in a black frame, there were names. Four thousand of them in total. Names of the Jewish martyrs who were deported and killed from my hometown, Pécs. As I read the familiar names, a kaleidoscope of pictures ran through my mind.

I looked up my father's name first, Szalai Ignácz (in the Hungarian language, surnames usually precede first names). I saw myself as a little girl in our small tinsmith shop. I had liked to watch my father's skilful hands work as he made cans, buckets, cake pans and other household items from tin. The whole city had known him for his honesty, integrity and diligence.

When the Jewish community sent me *Book of Tears* at my request, it included the following note: *The president of the Jewish community of Pécs remembers your father very well. He even remembers that there were three steps to enter your father's shop.* I was very touched that after so many decades people still remembered my father.

I read the next name, my mother's: Szalai Laura. In my mind's eye, I saw a small woman, a little on the plump side, whose dark hair had just started to turn grey. She had worked so hard all her life, taking care of the household, raising five daughters and helping out in Father's little shop. Just when she should have been starting to have an easier life after the last of her daughters got married, Mother was taken away with the rest of the Jewish inhabitants of Pécs.

The next few names in the book are Stern Miksa, that of his wife and four of their five children – Tibor, Zoltán, Éva and my best friend, Gizi. In 1943, during a visit to my parents with my baby son, we took an excursion with the Stern family. While we ate our lunch, we talked about children, among other topics. Suddenly six-year-old Éva remarked, "I know how babies are born."

"How do you know, darling? Would you tell me?" I asked the little girl. Then I added, "I would like to know also."

"I found out from the big book with many pictures in it, which is on the shelf," Eva replied. Then, looking around, she pointed to my infant son and said in a hushed voice, "I can't tell you now because the baby would overhear."

Turning the page, I saw the name Dr. Sebők Sándor. He was the boy who had escorted me home once and won my mother's heart with his simple acceptance of the watermelon she offered him.

Then I saw my older sister's name, Margaret. She had had such a short-lived happiness with Joe Halmos, but couldn't marry him because he was a gentile. My sister Ilona's name appears next. She had been happily married and was only thirty-nine years old when she was murdered. Then comes Ilona's son's name, George. George had been only eighteen years old when he was deported. When the Americans liberated the camp he was in, they separated the very sick and those with diarrhea from the others. George had the latter. One night, George snuck out of his room and stole some food. His starved stomach couldn't tolerate the food he ate, and he died the next morning.

The next familiar name in the book was that of Dr. Wallenstein Zoltán. He had been the chief rabbi of Pécs and the most handsome man I ever saw. At thirteen, I was very much in love with him. I can still hear his deep-toned voice as he recited a prayer to a group of young girls all in white at our b'nai mitzvah.

I read on. Ernest Géza. He had been our cantor, with a clear, silver-toned voice. I could have listened to him for hours. I still treasure one of his records with the beautiful melody of Kol Nidre, the opening prayer recited on the highest Jewish holy day, Yom Kippur.

Thousands of names. Thousands of memories.

Epilogue

In the early spring of 1989, when I received an invitation from the Jewish community of Pécs for its forty-fifth commemoration of the deportation of its four thousand Jewish citizens, I had a strong urge to go. I felt that I owed it to the memory of my parents to say a prayer at the martyrs' monument in the Pécs cemetery.

My husband and I arrived in Pécs from Budapest on June 30. Stepping down from the train, I had very mixed feelings at seeing my birthplace after more than forty years. First, we went to the Jewish community office, where they welcomed us warmly and told us about the services. It was still early in the afternoon, so I took my camera and went to see our small, old family house at 17 Alsóhavi utca. I had even planned to ask permission from the present owner to go in and look around the house of my childhood. With a throbbing heart, I finally reached the familiar street, but there was no number 17. All the houses from numbers 9 to 17 were in ruins.

Standing there, I recalled our small house with its three windows facing the street, the two high steps that led to the heavy door and the bell on the side, which rang many times a day because children liked to ring it just for fun. A woman passing by asked if I was looking for someone. "Yes," I replied. "I'm looking for my past." Then I asked about the houses, and she told me that the city had torn them down about four years before and still hadn't cleaned up the remains.

I turned and walked over to my father's small tinsmith shop on Irányi Dániel Square. I didn't have much luck there either. Where the shop had once stood, I found only new apartment buildings and a big patch of bare ground. In my mind's eye, I saw my father's store with him working diligently and skilfully inside.

I slowly turned and walked toward the synagogue and the Jewish elementary school next door. The school had become a Catholic college, and the synagogue was a tourist attraction during the summer. The synagogue still belonged to the Jewish community, but it was used for religious services only on High Holidays and special occasions.

There was a small prayer house beside the synagogue. My husband, Emil, and I went to the Friday night service there. We found about twenty-five worshippers from a remaining population of less than two hundred Jews. There was a cantor but no rabbi. A rabbi came to Pécs from Budapest every second week for the Sabbath service.

On Sunday morning, we visited a building that had been the Jewish ghetto on the outskirts of the city. This huge building, which resembled a military barracks, had once been home to railway employees and their families before the ghetto and now was home to these railway workers again. On this Sunday, representatives of the city and province and the railway workers placed wreaths at the site and said a few words. Then the rabbi made a short speech, and he and members of the Jewish community also placed a wreath, which was decorated with ribbons in blue and white, the colours of the flag of Israel.

After the ceremony, I stepped into the courtyard of the building behind the gate. I looked up at the small windows, wondering which room my parents, two sisters and their families might have squeezed into before they were taken away in cattle cars on their long and horrific ride to the gas chambers. I felt completely alone as I leaned on the wall, buried my face in my palms and cried my heart out.

On the same afternoon, a memorial service took place in the synagogue. In his speech, the rabbi said, "In this beautiful synagogue, which was full of worshippers before the Holocaust, only a few of us remain. Unfortunately, we can't fill the synagogue any more." As I listened, I envisioned the synagogue many decades before, full of worshippers on Friday nights, Saturday mornings and High Holidays. Returning to the present, I was surprised to hear the rabbi, in his mournful speech, quote from a famous poem that Hungarians often recite after singing the national anthem. The poem, entitled "Appeal," was written by Mihály Vörösmarty, a writer revered by most Hungarians. However, we Hungarian Jews could no longer relate to the verses.

> *Be true to the land of thy birth,*
> *Son of the Magyar race;*
> *It gave thee life, and soon its earth*
> *Will be thy resting place.*
>
> *Although the world is very wide,*
> *This is thy home;*
> *Come well or woe on fortune's tide;*
> *Here thou must live and die.*

Translated by W. Jaffray

The rabbi finished with his own words. "Not only did they not let us live in our country, they even sent us somewhere else to die." After the speech, the rabbi and cantor took out a large, black-covered book from under a glass in front of the Torah cabinet. It was the original copy of the *Book of Tears*, the book I had received. The rabbi read the opening words:

The Book of Tears *was written for future generations, to keep the names of the community's martyrs, those who were killed by fire, water, starvation, plagues and by the merciless and cruel hands of their fellow human beings during the Holocaust in the years 1940–1945. God must bring judgement over those evil ones who shed the blood of innocents.*

After the service, there were two buses waiting to take us to the cemetery. At the cemetery, we gathered around a monument that was a small replica of the Wailing Wall in Jerusalem. The inscription on it read:

The city of Pécs' remaining Jewish population mourns for their four thousand deported brothers and sisters. Pregnant young mothers with their children under their hearts, tiny babies, school-age boys and girls, teenage youngsters, God's rose garden of beautiful children, mothers and fathers, strong and weak, old and sick were dropped with tremendous suffering and humiliation into death.

In front of the monument, a black flag swayed in the light wind and mourners placed flowers at the base of the monument as the rabbi said Kaddish, the prayer for the dead.

The next morning, we left my hometown, which held so many sad memories. But I was glad that I had gone back because, in attending the services, I had made a bit of peace with myself. I felt I had come to a late funeral for my loved ones, a funeral that had never been possible for all those killed in Auschwitz.

Andy Réti

To the memory of my mother, whose love was unconditional and whose spirit was indomitable. To the memory of my beloved Magdi, who had a magnificent heart and a beautiful soul. Before she passed away in the year 2000, I read her my story, chapter by chapter. To my children, David and Kati, whom I love no matter what. To our late Papa, Emil. To the memory of my martyred father. To my maternal grandparents, whom I never knew. To my devoted Nagypapa and Nagymama, my paternal grandparents, who helped to raise me. To my wife, Judy. To the memory of six million brothers and sisters.

Acknowledgements

The credit belongs to the man who is actually in the arena ... who knows great enthusiasms, the great devotions; who spends himself in a worthy cause; who at the best knows in the end the triumph of high achievement, and who at the worst, if he fails, at least fails while daring greatly, so that his place shall never be with those cold and timid souls who neither know victory nor defeat.

> *Theodore Roosevelt*

No one stands alone. There are always people who care and are willing to help. I am fortunate to know a number of such people. The transformation of manuscript into book couldn't have been achieved without my editors, friends and family. The team included professionals and amateurs: my son, David, as well as Lucien Curnew, Josie Sipione, Alvin Abram, Tina Meale, Sherry Lalonde, Morton Roseman, Sandy Weisberg, Marian Gibson, Professor Marlene Kadar, Frank Diamant and, of course, my beloved Magdi. As of 2015, the team also includes the great people at the Azrieli Foundation. A very special thank you to editors Karen Kligman and Arielle Berger for doing such an incredible job of combining two books into one.

We are in the arena together.

Author's Preface

After my mother, Ibolya (Ibi) Grossman, took early retirement from her job at the Bank of Montreal, she took a course in creative writing. She showed me several of the stories she wrote, and I thought they were quite good. Since some of them dealt with our family and our own history, I suggested that she compile them in a booklet for her grandchildren to read. It was a passing comment, which I soon forgot. I can't describe my surprise and pleasure when, in 1990, she invited me to her book launch celebration and asked me to bring my camera to take some photographs! She'd kept the whole project such a secret that even during the editing process, our family was unaware of it.

On June 13, 1991, the Jewish Book Council's annual book awards presentation was held at the offices of the Jewish Federation of Greater Toronto. Our whole family and many friends attended this milestone event. The winning book for the category of Holocaust literature and the recipient of the Joseph Tanenbaum Holocaust Book Award was *An Ordinary Woman in Extraordinary Times*, published by the Multicultural History Society of Ontario. The author was my mother.

Introducing my mother, the presenter said, "Your memoir was chosen for its beautifully moving evocation of those difficult times and for its depiction of the indomitable spirit of the Jewish people in their struggle to survive and to tell their stories."

My mother's memoir depicts the tragedy that affected our lives, but it also shows that my mother didn't passively let things happen to us. Instead, she took charge whenever she could and, ultimately, triumphed. I was very proud of my mother as I listened to every word that was said about her and her book. Then the speaker said something that affected me profoundly. "There is a book in all of us, a story that is crying to get out and be told. We all have a story to tell." He was right. I also had a story to tell. I made up my mind right then and there to write my story.

Unbeknownst to me, my mother wrote her story because of me, and equally unbeknownst to her, she is the reason I've written this story. My story is a complement to my mother's book. It is a tribute to my mother and her indomitable spirit. There is no question in my mind that my life has been shaped not only by events that took place before I was born, but also greatly by my mother and our circumstances due to the extraordinary times we lived in. My mother's choices were limited. Nevertheless, she made it possible for me and, by extension, my children, to grow up in Canada – a wonderful place and a truly free country. The opportunities for me growing up in Canada were far-reaching, and for my children, born in Canada, the sky was the limit.

In the introduction to my mother's book, Professor Gabriele Scardellato wrote:

Mrs. Grossman carried, and did so with remarkable strength, the dual burden of her widowhood and her responsibility for her son. The presence of parents in various immigrations, Hungarian or other, is not unusual. The presence of single females, to say nothing of mothers and especially single mothers, is far less usual. Clearly, Mrs. Grossman's decision to find a better future for her son and herself deserves to be noted for the wonderful courage that it required.

In 1990, when my mother finished her book she wrote, "I pray and hope that the good Lord will give me some more years in good health so that I will be able to see my grandchildren grow to be decent Canadians with professions of their own choosing and liking." Her wish was granted, although she did not live to see the marriages of her beloved David and Kati, both in 2013. Ibi passed away on February 26, 2005. It was one of my greatest pleasures that I was able to present the first draft of my story to her while she was still alive. I did this on my birthday and according to her, "It was the greatest birthday gift a mother could get."

I feel that our stories should be read together. However, if either story positively influences just one mind or inspires one good deed, then we have succeeded. Like most things in life, a story is better when it is shared.

So, allow me to share my story.

What's in a Name?

I was born as Rechnitzer András on July 16, 1942, in Budapest, Hungary. Although I was born during World War II, the horrors had not yet fully reached us. In accordance with Jewish tradition, I was also given a Hebrew name, Hillel ben Menashe, which means "Hillel, son of Menashe." It is said that before naming a child after a specific person or relative, one has to be sure that that person lived a happy, fulfilling life. Hillel was a wise sage and teacher. I cannot comment on whether I am a wise man, but I have always felt comfortable teaching and sharing my knowledge with others.

The name Rechnitzer means "from the village of Rechnitz." I hope to visit that village sometime. Although Rechnitz is located in Austria, it was once part of Hungary and was called Rohonc. When I was three years old, my surname was changed to Réti, Hungarian for "of the field." I found out much later that many Hungarian Jews changed their names to sound more Hungarian, in order to assimilate and not be singled out as being Jewish.

When we came to Canada, András became Andrew, but I am known to all as Andy. András was the Hungarian version of Andreas, from Greek, meaning "manly." I believe my mother simply liked the name. My interpretation of "manly" was of being large or tall. Interestingly, I am neither particularly tall nor large, because I stopped growing at age fourteen. Much later, we found out that I was meant to be bigger and taller, as my father and grandfather were. However, when I was fourteen, half of my thyroid was removed due to the sudden growth of a cyst. With proper medication, I could have continued to grow. Unfortunately, medical knowledge was not as advanced in 1957 as it is today.

Nonetheless, I've never considered myself to be small nor allowed anyone to push me around. I have always thought of myself as a fighter. As it turned out, I fought for many causes, and losing was never an option. I must emphasize, however, that I was never alone in any of my fights.

During my childhood, both of my grandparents had a great influence on me. I remember many of my grandmother's folksy and wise sayings. One favourite was that she knew that a fight had started when I hit back. She was right. During my whole life, all my fights have started when I hit back. I was fortunate that I could always handle myself in a confrontation. Sometimes, I was too fearless. I am convinced that I was blessed with this ability for a reason. I was certainly not a street brawler or someone who walked around with a chip on his shoulder. I was involved in very few physical confrontations, but in many verbal and mental challenges, especially in my adult life. All of them started because I refused to back off whenever I was confronted with what I perceived to be an injustice. I hit back.

Although I can still hear my grandmother's words, in reality it was my mother who inspired me to fight for justice all my life. I know that many times I scared her, but I always tried to fight for the common good, and not for selfish reasons.

I am a positive person. Because I survived a horrific period in history, my choice is always to look at the bright side of things. There had to be a reason my mother and I survived while others on either side of us were killed. I went through some difficult times before I could accept God, but I believe that God helped us through the horrors of the Holocaust. I think the words of Holocaust survivor and Nobel Peace Prize Laureate Elie Wiesel sum up my feelings with great simplicity and eloquence: "The question is not, 'Where was God?' but 'Where was Man?'"

The concept of God was very difficult for me to comprehend and come to terms with. As an adult, I know a lot of things I didn't know before. I know that God was with us and is within all of us. Only upon becoming an adult was I able to understand what had happened to my family and me when I was a child. As an adult, I know that, as human beings, we always have choices in life. The ability to choose is one of the truly great gifts from God. It is up to each individual to do good or evil. I believe in God and the essence of goodness in humanity.

My life was easier and happier than my mother's. In fact, I had a wonderful childhood. My devoted paternal grandparents and my mother provided me with love and as much material comfort as their meagre incomes could provide. They all did their very best to compensate for the missing element in our lives, my father. I remember my paternal grandmother sitting in front of our stove, crying silently, with only her shoulders moving up and down. Only once did I ever hear her cry out loud and ask, "Why couldn't you take me? Why did you have to take my son?" I must admit that I cried about this scene only some fifty years later – in fact, as I wrote my story.

It was much later in my life that it became difficult for me to accept that I had grown up without a father and had had to live without the ties that I have with my beloved children, David and Kati. I wanted to know why my father was taken. It was a long time before I could live with this burning question. It was a strange feeling to grow up without a father, especially to have known all my adult life that his only crime was that he was Jewish. Whenever I could, I tried to find an answer to Why? How? How could anyone let this happen? I wanted all my bottled-up emotions to have an outlet.

As far back as I can remember, I had been told that my father died of typhus due to the horrible conditions in the camps. I had read the letter my mother wrote in 1945, but she had never given me the one addressed to me when I was older, which she wrote in 1946. All the stories I had heard about my father indicated that he was an athlete in his prime, in good physical and mental health. I could not believe that he would succumb to a disease.

In the 1970s, my mother discovered a first cousin of my father's, Baba, who was living in Toronto. This kind of encounter was quite common among survivors. We were scattered around the four corners of the earth after the Holocaust. We found out that Baba's brother, Harry, had been in the same unit as my father. Harry was living in Belgium, and he came to Toronto for my son's bar mitzvah in 1984. These people were relatives that I hadn't known we had, but I took an immediate liking to Harry. Somehow, I happened to mention to him the feelings I had about my father's death, that he must have been murdered. Harry looked me in the eye and told me that I was right – my father had not died from typhus. It felt very strange to speak to an eyewitness. Learning the truth about my father during this time was inexplicably reassuring for me.

Their unit was one of many in a forced labour battalion, digging ditches and fortifications. They were forced to work and exist in sub-human conditions on very little food. Most of the unit survived almost until the end, including my father. They could already hear the advancing Soviets. Harry was not married, while most others, like my father, were young family men. Harry asked my father to escape with him. My father told Harry that he could not risk trying to escape, because they would be shot on the spot if they were captured. He said that he had a family counting on him. For our sake, he could not take the risk. He just wanted to survive. He told Harry that he had Ibi and András waiting for his return. Harry described his escape to me; he said that he only got far enough to hide behind some bushes when he heard the machine guns.

I have visited my father's memorial in Budapest three times since 1956. His cherished memory is alive. To know that he died because he loved us gives me strength and resolve.

My Formative Years

From the day I was born until the day we left for Canada, we lived at Népszinház utca (Folk Theatre Street) 16, f5, Budapest, Hungary. Where I lived is significant in many ways, mostly because of the lifestyle or conditions under which we were forced to live. As children, we are all blessed with a certain innocence, enthusiasm and wonderment. I had a good life considering my circumstances. We were poor, like all others around us, but, as a child, I didn't know that.

The place was a vertical village – literally. The structure of the building was so different from what is known to us in North America. It included what we call an "atrium." There were actually two separate buildings mirroring each other and built around an open courtyard, with all the apartments opening from the circular corridors. As a result, we saw our neighbours and knew one another. We were not isolated.

Our apartment was the first one on the street level. It consisted of two rooms, plus a kitchen and a storage room with a toilet installed by my father before he was taken away to a labour camp. We had no bathroom or central heating, and only cold running water. A small coal-burning stove located in the first room was the only source of heat, and it was too small to heat the whole place. We hardly used the kitchen because my grandmother used it as a storage shed for coal and wood.

The apartment building had a labyrinth of a basement where everybody had lockers for their coal. I think that my grandmother, who came from a rural village and was superstitious in many ways, was not willing to go down into that dark, musty place. I don't think she was afraid for herself, but for me. She tried to avoid taking me there, since I tagged along wherever she went. I know for a fact that kids, and even adults, got lost down there at times. The basement stretched out for a long distance, even under the neighbouring apartment building. I spent a lot of good times, both alone and with others, exploring that labyrinth and the equally fascinating attic. Nobody told me that I was supposed to be afraid of the dark. Our home influenced me in many ways, perhaps most importantly in making me very independent.

The recovery from the war and the switch to a communist system of government affected every person living in Hungary following the country's full liberation on April 4, 1945. During the siege of Budapest, apartments had been bombed out or rendered uninhabitable. There were shortages of everything – from food to coal and medicine. Under the communist government, a bureaucratic central registry system assigned people to live together even if they were total strangers. Our apartment building had various types and sizes of units. We were lucky that we could live with my grandparents, no matter how cramped the unit was.

Our apartment had no direct sunlight. For a brief time in the late afternoon, the reflection from the third-floor apartment window hit the top of our apartment. Except for this very small area with the bright sunlight, the rest was always dark. Electricity cost money we didn't have. No one I knew had a television. I didn't even lay eyes on one until we came to Canada.

I spent a great deal of time outside, on the stoop of our apartment, reading. I loved reading, and I read as much as I could. One of the things my grandfather taught me was to think of books as my friends. Sitting outside also offered interesting encounters. There was an elderly blind man who lived in the building opposite ours. He passed by regularly, and I always escorted him. I learned at an early age to respect people who were elderly or had a physical disability and to offer them my seat on a streetcar or bus.

I also learned to observe the world. My world was small at the time, but I could be part of it or keep away from it when it suited me. Even at a young age, I never had any problem being part of a group, with either children or adults. I could always fit in. Much later in life, I heard the credo "Lead, follow or get out of the way." I believe that I started practising this at a very early age.

Necessity is a great master. From the time I was eight years old, I was on my own all day long. My mother and grandfather were working, and for a time my grandmother also took on a full-time job. I was a latchkey kid; I carried the key to our apartment on a string around my neck tucked under my shirt. I never felt abandoned. I was very self-assured and knew I was trusted and able to do things on my own. I became very good at heating up leftovers, that is, after I burnt holes in the bottoms of two pots. At the time, my grandmother was working in the kitchen of a large school, and sometimes I went there to eat. We didn't have much food, and there was no option to eat anything other than what was left for me. We often ate leftovers. I can still hear my grandmother's dictum, "All food to be eaten, nothing left to be rotten."

I was welcome in the homes of all my friends, and I loved visiting them. All my friends had better apartments than ours, with regular kitchens and bathrooms. Most of them even had an icebox. I especially enjoyed visiting the home of my best friend, Ivan, who lived on the second floor. His family was a little better off than mine was, and his live-in grandmother cooked and baked for his family all the time. Ivan and his younger sister, Susie, were a little bit spoiled and had the tendency to be picky eaters. I loved their grandmother, Zseni *néni*. There was nothing that she offered me that wasn't "the best I ever ate," especially her *lekváros bukta*, sweet buns filled with jam. I was never too shy to accept anything that was offered to me, and I learned the power of saying thank you at an early age.

～

I was introduced to swimming at the age of five. My mother was always worried that I would overdo things, and when I later started to train seriously for competitive swimming, I woke up without an alarm clock and left the house at 5:30 a.m. without waking up anyone else. I had heard about the power of self-suggestion. I just repeated to myself a number of times that I wanted to get up at five in the morning, and I always did.

I guess swimming was in my genes, since both my father and grandfather were excellent swimmers and swimming instructors. My grandfather was also a renowned podiatrist and masseur, and he taught both subjects and had even written a book on podiatry. He became the manager of the leading health spa in Hungary, the Palatinus, and I spent many summer days there. The Palatinus was on Margaret Island on the Danube River, between the twin cities of Buda and Pest. It was a huge place, even by our North American standards: it had a pool that was more than one hundred metres long, an artificial wave pool, a huge picnic area and a big, circular, therapeutic, natural hot-spring pool.

For me, this place was strictly for fun. A few other key personnel were allowed to have their kids there, and the bunch of us had a great time. I was the only one allowed to help with cleaning the pool and ringing the bell announcing the start of the waves in the artificial wave pool. The job was a great privilege. I loved to see all the people flock to the pool on my command. The cleaning involved completely draining the wave pool and hosing it down on a regular basis. I don't think the pool had a filtration system. In those days, people had bathing suits with pockets. Consequently, we cleared a lot of money, combs and sunglasses from the bottom of the pool. We turned in the articles to the lost and found, but kept the money. Finders keepers. I also got a small allowance from my grandfather. Although there were ice cream and pastry vendors at the Palatinus, I spent my money sparingly. I was saving to buy a camera.

My competitive swim training took place adjacent to the Palatinus at the National Swim Centre. It was the breeding ground of many Olympic and world champions. I felt at home there. After a while, I was given an honorary pass to the Swim Centre. This great privilege was usually reserved for the elite national selects. I got this great honour on merit. Swimming proved beneficial to me for the rest of my life. It taught me discipline and perseverance. It instilled in me the ideal of a healthy body and mind.

When I was thirteen, I spent the summer with my uncle Jenö about an hour south of Budapest. I adored my uncle. He was very smart, had a doctorate in economics and was in charge of a large construction project: the building of a brand new city for the steel and iron industry from the ground up on the shores of the Danube, to be called Stalin City. The city was renamed after the Hungarian Revolution, and is now called Dunaújváros.

My uncle knew of my independent streak and allowed me to go wherever I wanted. He even provided me with a bicycle. My bicycle and I were inseparable, until a four-metre cliff came between us. It was a serious accident. I dislocated my right hip and severely strained and bruised my spine. The doctor said that I might never walk properly again. But God was with me, and my grandmother was convinced that my father was also looking after me. My swim training, my treasured honorary pass at the National Swim Centre and my grandfather's connections also helped a great deal. Being in possession of the honorary pass allowed me admission and treatment at the National Sports Medical Institute, which was staffed by the best doctors and physiotherapists in the country and intended to serve only the elite national athletes.

After the initial treatment, I didn't show much improvement. I could drag my foot, but I couldn't walk on it. I asked the doctors if I could go swimming, and they told me that if I could get to the pool, then I should go ahead. I was determined and inspired by Olivér

Halassy, a former Hungarian Olympic champion who had won a gold medal even though he had only one foot. I was on crutches for a long time, and that is how I made my way to the pool. It took a while, but I healed without any permanent damage. With all my heart, I wanted to be an Olympian. In my mind, I still am. I know that participation is just as important as winning. My whole life I tried to live by the Olympic ideal *Citius, Altius, Fortius,* which is Latin and translates to Swifter, Higher, Stronger.

At age fourteen, I won a national championship for my age group. The year was 1956 – the year of the October revolution, the year we left Hungary, the end of my competitive swimming career.

Communism and Religion

The communist government tried to dictate every aspect of everyone's lives in Hungary and demanded blind obedience. They mimicked the Soviets in everything, including their stance on religion. According to the Soviets, who were officially atheists, religion had to be eradicated everywhere, especially in their new empire behind the Iron Curtain.

All youth, including me, were members of the Young Pioneers, an organization imported from the Soviet Union, which was the first step on the road leading to admission into the Communist Party. The organization was similar to Boy Scouts, except for the political indoctrination that Stalin was our father figure. Stalin's picture and statue were everywhere. We also had to memorize his "wise utterings."

The advantage of the communist system for children was that everything was sponsored by the state and therefore free. We were all encouraged to participate in many activities. Boy oh boy, did I participate! I was a member of the photography club, chess club, model airplane club, ping-pong club, stamp collecting club and folk dance club. We all played soccer, the national pastime. The glee club was definitely out (people actually begged me to stay out).

My grandfather was a willing communist, a party functionary. He believed in the party line of official atheism, and because of this my religious training was minimal. I loved and adored my grandfather. If something wasn't important for him, then it wasn't important for me either. The connection between my father's murder and our Judaism did not occur to me until later in my life. My mother and grandmother had some very serious arguments with my grandfather on the subject of religion. I did have a bar mitzvah, but my grandfather did not attend.

My grandfather was a very intelligent man. He spent a great deal of time with me, and I learned many things from him. One interesting learning experience was the process of self-criticism, which was part of the communist doctrine. I learned to look at my actions and their possible consequences with a critical eye. This process made me try harder at everything I did, but it also eroded some of my natural self-confidence.

To understand and be a part of history in the making requires a little more maturity and knowledge than I possessed at age fourteen. Although my favourite subject in school was history, my knowledge of it at the time had some great, gaping holes. I didn't have the faintest understanding that the Soviets, whose system was forced on Hungary, were not our "liberators" but our jailers.

This lack of information was further complicated by the revisionist history we were obliged to swallow. I knew all about the heroic struggles of the Soviet army against the Nazi hordes, the battle of Stalingrad, the inventions that came from the minds of the great proletariat of the Soviets and the works of Marx, Engels, Stalin and Lenin. However, I had absolutely no idea that World War II was not exclusively between the Germans and the Soviets. It never occurred to me that if it was a world war, then the United States, Canada, England and other nations might have been involved as well.

Students protesting against the communist system started the 1956 Hungarian revolution. When the demonstrations and protests started to take place, I did not join for a number of reasons. My mother was beside herself with fear and begged me to stay inside. My grandfather also stayed home and didn't let me out of his sight, but, most importantly, I had no reason to protest against anything. I felt that I didn't have any problems. Being ignorant at that time had its advantages, but I can say with conviction that later, in my adult life, I fought against ignorance whenever and wherever I came upon it.

The revolution forced us to change our daily lives and, as it turned out, the rest of our lives. When my grandfather and I were out to buy some food one day, a group of armed protestors came out from a side street as a Soviet tank came rumbling toward us from a distance. My grandfather grabbed me, and we ducked behind the open door of a building. One of the armed protestors tried to throw a Molotov cocktail at the tank, but the fight was over in seconds; the machine gunfire from the tank was deadly accurate. I recognized the fallen young hero; he was my classmate Balázs. Still clutching his gun, he lay dead as the other protestors ran off.

The tank never stopped or slowed down. It simply continued down the street, a great mechanical beast that had just crushed an ant, not caring about it one way or another. On another occasion, a Soviet tank sent in to crush the revolution was stationed directly in front of our building, shelling some target. The big shells were left on the street when the tank moved off. Up until then, I had never even seen a gun or a bullet other than in movies. In addition, there were some regular bullet casings scattered all over the street.

Our building was not targeted or shot at because we did not have anybody shooting or throwing grenades at the Soviets. Nevertheless, being shelled or bombed was a real possibility. Our small apartment was located on the ground level, a location considered relatively safe in the event of bombing. As a result, we had four other families move in with us from the higher floors. I don't remember any of them. Under those conditions, I found a solution that worked for me: I slept a lot.

During breaks in the shooting, the adults went out in search of food and the kids went out to play. The shells and bullets made great toys. I thought that one large tank shell would make a great flower vase. The irony of it was lost on me for a long time. My mother remembers the following story differently, but I am certain it happened like this: One day, out of nowhere, two soldiers burst into our apartment with their guns at the ready. I was the closest to the door. One of the soldiers was Mongolian, not Soviet. His eyes were fierce, his gun was pointed and he was ready to shoot first and ask questions later. When he saw the throng of humanity in the small apartment, he looked even more ready; his body language was unmistakable. He seemed just as worried about getting shot as we were. He glanced around but did not say a word until he saw the tank shell and some small bullet casings next to it. Then he demanded, in Russian, who had the gun.

We had had to learn Russian in school, but I seldom learned things that were forced on me, and our Russian teacher was a former French teacher who was only a couple of lessons ahead of us. My ability to speak Russian was definitely lacking, but this soldier was definitely ready to shoot unless he got an answer – I could see it in his eyes. My Russian came to me in a rush. I was able to explain to him that nobody had a gun and that the empty shell was only a toy for the children. He saw the group of kids, lowered his gun and looked around the apartment. Years later, I found out that one of the people who had stayed with us was a secret service detective who had hidden his pistol in a drainpipe. Ignorance truly is bliss.

While one soldier searched the place, the other soldier left. I found out why a few minutes later. The soldier who left went to some of the other apartments and rounded up a group of men, including my grandfather, who was just coming home. Neither my mother nor my grandmother was aware of what was happening until we saw the men being taken away. I still don't know how both of them were able to maintain their composure while watching my grandfather being taken away again, only a few years after the wartime horrors of the recent past.

Since I was the closest to the door, I was able to speak to my grandfather as he was being led away. He assured me that he and the others would be back shortly. They were being taken to headquarters for questioning by the Soviet leaders. Having one soldier remain with us was a relatively good sign that my grandfather would come back. The soldier asked for a glass of water but made me take the first sip before he drank it. Then he asked me to tell him what city he was in, which surprised me. The soldier thought he was in the city of Suez. He showed me his watch, which gave the time at his home base somewhere inside the Soviet Union.

I was not afraid, and I did not feel like a hostage. Some years back, near where I now stood, I had gotten a piece of bread from a Soviet soldier just before our liberation. To this day, I can remember how that piece of bread tasted and that it quelled my extreme hunger. It was that kind act that made me unafraid now. My mother's beautiful poem captured that memory:

HUNGER

"Mommy, mommy, please give me a little piece of bread. I am hungry, very hungry! Just this little, mommy!" My two-year-old son put his two tiny fingers together showing just how little he wanted.

"Tomorrow, my son, tomorrow maybe the war will be over and you will have all the bread you want. Hush, hush, little one. Go to sleep. Don't cry. Mommy will hold you, my darling, and sing you a lullaby."

The next day comes and goes, but no food, only hopes. Hopes that tomorrow we could be free. The following morning indeed, we hear noises, different voices. We all rush to the courtyard, and there he is – a Russian soldier who just liberated us.

I beg him with sign language, with tears running on my

cheeks, "Please give me some bread. My baby is starving to death." The soldier reaches into his pocket and puts a roll in my hand. As I give it to my child, he looks at it with wide, unbelieving eyes. Then, crying and laughing and jumping with joy, he bites into the soft, beautiful white roll.

Ibolya Grossman

My trust in Soviet soldiers was further enhanced by the communist school system. For more than seven years, I had been indoctrinated to believe that the Soviet people fought for the rights of the working class. Wasn't my family proletarian working class? Were we not friends? Were we not on the same side? How young and naïve I was! My youth and my extreme naïveté came to an end just a few weeks later.

My grandfather returned in about an hour's time. At headquarters, they had needed some information, and he was the official translator. My grandfather could speak Russian fluently, along with six other languages. When he came back home, we were immensely relieved. The other families moved back to their own apartments, because the immediate danger was over.

I found out later that being taken away by the Soviet soldier was the final straw that convinced my grandfather to abandon the Communist Party. This process had actually started for him in March of 1953, three years earlier, which was when Stalin died. Although I did not find out until much later what a monster and mass murderer Stalin was, I remember helping my grandfather burn all of Stalin's books, along with some other communist doctrines. By 1956, my grandfather had resigned from the Communist Party's secretariat and had stopped attending meetings.

During the protests, antisemitic graffiti was beginning to appear on the streets of Budapest, but this incident was a turning point. It made my grandfather realize that my mother and I had no future in communist Hungary. He loved me, so he let me go.

My mother described our escape, which of course it was, in her memoir. I looked upon it as a new adventure. After all, this was our second attempt already. When I was seven years old, we had tried to escape Hungary, but we had been captured and jailed.

The decision to leave was not forced on me. My mother raised me with great love and affection. In many things, she was ahead of her time, including child rearing. She did not treat me like a child but like a young adult. She explained the reasons we should leave and asked me if I wanted to go. We never discussed it seriously, but I have a feeling that if I had said no, she would have sacrificed everything and left without me.

My memory of the events and places is hazy by now. We stayed in Vienna and applied to go to the United States or Australia, where I knew they had great swimming programs. The application process and waiting time were long. One day we heard that the Canadian embassy was accepting applications and that we could leave for Canada immediately. By then my fourteen-year-old patience was exhausted, and I just wanted to get going.

On December 27, 1956, we boarded the MS *Berlin* and sailed for Canada. We embarked on a journey toward our new life, a life filled with surprises, obstacles, problems, pleasures and rewards.

The True North

I am very proud to be Canadian. Canadians' tolerance, compassion and willingness to help others are universally known. Canada's natural resources, industry and commerce constantly put it on the list of best places to live in the world.

However, I did not know any of this on January 7, 1957, the day we landed in Halifax, many years ago. The only thing I knew about Canada was that it was a dominion and that the Queen of England's picture was on every stamp, something I knew from my stamp collection. I did not know about Canada's vast area, cold winter temperatures, incredible northern beauty and wonderful people or about the richness of the English language.

At first, I had trouble learning English. My previous attempts at learning languages had been failures, but eventually English became second nature to me. At the time, I had no idea that later on I would be making some of my livelihood due to my skill with the language. Nor did I imagine that I would become a writer, reporter, columnist, recording secretary, instructor and public speaker. I love the English language, and just like my mother, I also use the dictionary as much as I can, but I use only the English version.

When we arrived in Halifax in 1957, Pier 21 was the port of entry for all new Canadians. We couldn't speak one word of English. We were placed in temporary quarters until we could be processed. Those who had relatives or friends already living in Canada were taken to their requested destination to join them. Those, like us, who knew no one in Canada, were given an assigned destination. Ours was Winnipeg.

The three-and-a-half-day train ride was incredible. The scenery, the excitement and the people on the train served as a fitting beginning for a new life. We couldn't believe that one could travel that long and still reach only halfway across Canada. The vastness was overwhelming. The landscape was breathtaking. We were in a cabin where the seats converted to a bed at night, but I did not sleep much. I was glued to the window. Everyone on the train treated us with great courtesy. The dining car was something I had read about in books; I had never expected to experience it first-hand!

When we arrived in Winnipeg, I thought we had arrived in a land of giants. From the train window, I noticed everybody wearing boots, but close up, because of the heavy clothing, they all looked bigger than they were. Then I saw a real giant – a police officer wearing the traditional buffalo coat and high hat.

It was a typical January day in Winnipeg, and we were standing at the corner of Portage and Main – often referred to as the coldest and windiest spot in Manitoba – where it was -40°C. In the summer, it reached 39°C in the shade (if you could find any). It was very cold, this Canada. The moment I ventured out the door, I found out very quickly why everybody was wrapped up. Luckily, I got frostbite on only one ear (it happened after only five minutes in the cold). We did not have proper warm clothing. What we had on our backs was what we had been wearing when we left Hungary, and that clothing was not meant for a Canadian winter.

In typical Canadian fashion, people generously came to our aid in no time at all. We spent about three weeks at Immigration Hall, where we were given regular meals and some basic necessities. After that, the Canadian Jewish Congress placed us in a basement apartment and provided us with all the basic necessities.

Sometimes, when I reflect back on those early days, I am truly amazed at what this country gave us. Knowing what I know today about all the things that could have happened to us, the life my mother achieved for us was truly a great accomplishment. Today, Winnipeg never reminds me of cold. I always remember it as a warm, hospitable and caring community.

Our basement apartment was never locked. When we asked the landlady for a key in our very broken English, she told us there was no key because the door did not have a lock. We found it a bit strange, but perhaps break-ins just did not happen in Winnipeg in 1957.

One day when I came home from school, I found what I thought was a huge snowdrift outside our door. It prevented me from getting into the house. Heavy snowfall was very common in Winnipeg. When I started to remove the snow, I discovered that it was actually a pile of clothing and household items that someone had left for us. We never found out who the kind donor was. Buried in the pile was a treasure that I used for so many years that my mother threatened to burn it unless I accepted a replacement. It was a beige wool naval overcoat with a hood and wooden buttons, just like the one worn by Jack Hawkins in the movie *The Cruel Sea*, which I had seen in Hungary. My "new" coat braced many winters with me.

My mother got a job as a sewing-machine operator in a factory, and I was sent to school. At first, I had some difficulty adjusting, but once I could speak the language, it became much easier. I also got a job as a delivery boy on a bicycle, for fifty cents an hour. Once I had warm clothes, I actually enjoyed my first part-time job. To this day, the crunch of dry snow in the evening is a very pleasant sound to me.

Once again, I saved my money to buy a camera. Just as I had done in swimming, I set goals for myself. Sadly, I did not have a chance to go near a swimming pool for some time, but I did swim across the Red River as soon as the weather turned warm. My mother had the same horrified reaction to this as when I had swum across the Danube River in Budapest about a year before, although that experience seemed like a lifetime ago.

~

In the neighbouring province of Ontario, the Jewish Camp Council ran a summer camp near Kenora. During my first summer in Canada, the council paid for my stay at the B'nai Brith camp for the whole summer. The camp was located on an island somewhere in the middle of Lake of the Woods and the only approach was by boat. As on the winter train ride, I was again exposed to the breathtaking beauty of the Canadian landscape. I did not hear of the Group of Seven artists for many years to come, but I came to love those rugged Canadian scenes that they painted so well because I experienced them first-hand during my first Canadian summer. And what a glorious summer it was!

I had my prized camera, which I had worked for all winter long. I fancied myself a photographer (I was fifteen and I had a camera, so what else could I be?) and went wild clicking away at all the scenery until I had no film left – until visitors' day, when my mother brought up another roll.

Strangely, it was the camera that caused one of my first culture clashes. I'd purchased it new and took it with me to camp in its original cardboard box. The camera was a combination of the old accordion folding style and newer technology. When we got to the campsite, we were told to put all of our hand luggage in one place and start unloading the suitcases and duffel bags. I was glad to be helping. After the first load, I discovered that my precious camera was being used as a marker to show where to pile the luggage. When I realized what was happening, I started digging for my treasure right away. I wasn't particularly concerned about what I threw and where it landed; I just wanted to get to my camera. Fortunately, the camera was sturdy enough and survived its ordeal. The shock came when everybody who gathered around me wanted to know what kind of radio it was. I didn't think it resembled a radio, but then, I had never seen a portable, battery-operated radio before.

The few cameras that other kids had were all Kodak Brownies. They had single-shot "point and click" mechanisms. None of my new friends had studied photography or knew the intricacies of lens settings, light and shadow, filters or shutter speed. None of them had ever developed their own negatives. They all took their exposed films to the drugstore and got back their snapshots in a week's time.

I had never been to a camp before, let alone a Jewish camp. This was my first exposure to the Jewish community as an entity, where Jewish existence, heritage and lifestyle were something to learn, to practise and to be proud of. I had never attended Sabbath services before, and experiencing it for the first time in my life was very moving. The service was even more memorable because it was conducted at a clearing overlooking a greenish-blue lake, under brilliant blue skies, highlighted by the rugged beauty of the northern topography. Seeing the rabbi conducting the service with the magnificent lake behind him is a beautiful memory. My lack of knowledge was amply made up for by my awe of the occasion and the enthusiasm of the others.

The beautiful Canadian landscape that I had watched from the train window just a few months earlier was now directly in front of me, next to me and around me, to be touched and enjoyed. The beauty of the place is etched in my mind permanently. It is also forever connected with the freedom that we sing about in our national anthem: "O Canada ... the True North strong and free." I learned the anthem along with many other new things at camp, including the realization that I liked girls, who were in a separate section. Not all the campers were from Winnipeg. It seemed that I made an impression on Anita, a young lady who lived in Flin Flon, Manitoba. She told me that she had relatives in Winnipeg, and in the fall when she visited her relatives, she wanted to take me to a dance.

At camp, my English rapidly improved, while my Jewish identity and deep roots to the Jewish community were brought to the surface. Camp offered a lot of interesting, exciting and adventurous experiences. I learned how to paddle a canoe. I discovered that you can add lake water to powder and turn it into milk, that some Jews eat kosher meals, and that I can't remember any song past the first two lines, but that it doesn't matter because I can't carry a tune anyway.

I had not been near a body of water to practise my swimming for a whole year. I was out of practice and out of shape. The waterfront was wonderful, but it was not set up for serious swimming. We could swim only during scheduled periods. We had an annual rivalry with a neighbouring camp, and the competition included an across-the-lake swim from our camp to theirs. Counsellors in boats followed us in case we ran into difficulty. Their task was reasonably easy, since most kids were all bunched together swimming in one group.

There are basically four strokes in competitive swimming: front crawl, backstroke, breaststroke and butterfly. An across-the-lake swim is usually done using front crawl. However, since I was a breast-stroke and butterfly specialist, my front crawl was weak. I started out doing the front crawl just like everyone else, but I got tired from it rather quickly. Without thinking, I switched to the breaststroke, which is known as a resting stroke. Unbeknownst to me, I started pulling ahead of the pack, and it took a while before a canoe caught up with me. The paddler told me that I shouldn't swim unattended. Well, it was his choice to stay with me or go back to the others, because I was not going to slow down! I finished the race way ahead of anybody else.

On the Move Again

By September, when school started, my mother and I were beginning to fit in and settle into a routine. At school, I had problems for a number of reasons, but mainly because of my unfamiliarity with English. I started out in Grade 8, which was only two years behind where I should have been, but in a very short time I was demoted to Grade 6. Then, I failed Grade 6 and was instructed to repeat it. At fifteen years old, I had no intention of doing that since I had already graduated from elementary school with honours in Hungary. Being a streetwise kid, I discovered at an early age that all problems have solutions. I eventually found a solution to my problem once we moved to Toronto.

My mother and I started planning our move to Toronto after her sister Aranka arrived with her family in Canada and settled there. We decided to move during the summer, once school was out. Since we were no longer newcomers, we took it for granted that we would do this second move entirely on our own. We did not expect any help, and I don't think we would have accepted any. We knew that we had to save up for our airfares and another settling-in period. I continued to work at part-time jobs while my mother worked at a factory.

In those early days, my keen sense of justice did not extend to the realization that my poor mother was working in a factory earning twenty-six dollars a week while, as a student summer worker, I was earning forty-two dollars a week as a shipper at the warehouse for Surplus Army, Air Force, Navy (S A A N), a large Western chain of discount family department stores. I loved this job, and I had obtained it from a relative stranger who just wanted to help my mother and me.

By the end of July 1958, just a few weeks after my sixteenth birthday, we had enough money saved to make the move to Toronto. We augmented our savings by selling some of our furniture. The experience I gained at the warehouse came in handy, because we were able to ship ahead our clothing. I could hardly wait; I was going to take my first-ever plane ride!

We left Winnipeg with just a bit more baggage than when we arrived. I was never a sentimental person. Leaving one place and going to another was no big deal. Of the many changes of address we had, I never had a favourite. They were just places to live, roofs over our heads.

In Toronto, we had a relatively short settling-in period. My uncle and aunt helped us as much as they could, but they had their own lives and struggles to deal with. Before school started, my mother found a job and an apartment in the Jewish neighbourhood – I think we settled into the Jewish area by accident. This was the beginning of my connection to Judaism, and the sights and smells of our new neighbourhood soon became familiar. Our home and its surroundings began to make me feel as if I belonged there.

At Central Technical School, I neglected to tell the administration that my previous school had put me in Grade 6, and I registered for Grade 11, where I should have been in the first place. When they asked for proof of my schooling, I showed them my Hungarian papers and explained that my Grade 8 was equivalent to their Grade 11.

Central Tech was one of the largest high schools in Toronto at the time. More than two thousand students were divided into two streams: a smaller general course stream and a much larger technical course stream. Most students there did not want to go on to higher education; they just wanted to learn a trade. The general course, which I took, was geared for entering university.

The school had incredible facilities, ones I couldn't have imagined in my wildest dreams, at least not where I had come from. It had several well-equipped shops, for example – automotive, aircraft, woodworking, and machine – rooms full of drafting tables, arts and crafts studios, a theatre, an auditorium, a rifle range and – my favourite – a swimming pool. I was told they had a swim team and that I could join it, but practice would not start for another month. I was astounded to learn that other schools had their own pools, too, some of which were even bigger. It was the longest month I ever had to wait, but I was back to swimming!

Central Tech is located at the corner of Bathurst and Harbord Streets, in the heart of a neighbourhood that had a large Jewish population. It was also close to both Spadina Avenue, the heart of the *shmatte*, or Jewish garment, district, and Bloor Street, lined with pool halls, cinemas and restaurants. The school was also very close to Harbord Collegiate, where the majority of the Jewish kids went. I didn't find out any of this until much later.

Bloor and Spadina was also the favourite hangout of Hungarian Torontonians. At the intersection of the two streets was my future home away from home, the Young Men's Hebrew Association – the YMHA, known as the Y – with a really good practice pool.

In 1958, Toronto had very little unemployment. I went from store to store asking if anyone needed an after-school helper, and I found a part-time job working for a dry goods wholesaler, a textile shop. I got the job on the strength of my experience working as a shipper and packer. My mother couldn't get over that I was in the *shmatte* business. The job was on Dundas Street, right next to the Jewish Market, as it was known, before it became Kensington Market.

Because Mr. Solnitsky, the owner, was an observant Jew, we were closed on Shabbat and other Jewish holidays. We sold a lot of sweaters, cardigans, underwear, socks and children's wear, which I knew how to fold, pack and load onto the delivery trucks. Since I also knew where all the merchandise was located, I sometimes acted as a salesperson. We were selling to small store owners – wholesale only, no retail.

Just as I had done previously, I gave my earnings to my mother and she gave me an allowance from it. As a result, I had spending money to go to the movies and restaurants or shoot pool with my friends, within limits of course. Without exception, I made all my friends on Bloor Street, on Spadina Avenue or at the Y. One day, while walking along Bloor, I bumped into Mike Andrádi, my childhood friend and former classmate from Hungary. Our friendship went all the way back to kindergarten.

As it turned out, the majority of my classmates had fled from Hungary, and many of them had come to Canada and ended up in either Toronto or Montreal. In no time at all, I found all those who lived in Toronto. We started hanging out at the Y on a regular basis. The Y was the hub of activity for all of us immigrants. At the Y, I also made new friends, including David, who was originally from Poland and became a lifelong friend. My core group of friends consisted of me, David and my three classmates from Bezerédy elementary school in Budapest – Mike (Miklós), Irwin (Ervin) and Julius (Gyuszi). We were the "Hungarian" contingent at the Y, with David acquiring an honorary Hungarian status. I believe that our becoming Canadian-ized began with the simple act of changing our names and accelerated as we spoke English more and more, even among ourselves.

I also met many Canadian kids. The new acquaintances included the young ladies my friends and I escorted to dances and parties. Our large group spent all our leisure time together. The group eventually swelled to as many as thirty. I was the only one in our group who still attended school at the time. The others all had jobs and worked hard. In spite of the temptations of the money that all my friends were making, I had no intention of quitting school. Actually, I liked school, and Central Tech was a great school to attend. The previous holes in my education were beginning to be filled in, like the gaps in my knowledge about the events of World War II. I also learned about Canadian history and heritage. English literature was one of my fa-vourite subjects. Due to my accent, I was assigned to read the part of

Eliza when we studied *Pygmalion* (the play that was made into the movie *My Fair Lady*). As for extracurricular activities, in addition to being on the swim team, I played on the school's soccer team and occasionally wrote articles for the school newspaper.

My friend Mike, who is one of the most generous and good-hearted people I know, lent me his prized possession one day, a 1954 Mercury convertible with a four-barrel carburetor, a four-on-the-floor and an overdrive. On a beautiful spring afternoon, six of my friends and I piled into the car for a drive – before classes were over. The vice-principal called me into his office the next day and asked me to explain my absence. Since my overall attendance was pretty good and the vice-principal had four other students waiting, he just told me not to skip classes again. It was an easy promise to keep; it was my last year at Central Tech.

While I was still in school, my mother met a wonderful man, Emil Grossman. My mother asked my opinion about Emil before she married him in 1958. I told her I liked him, which I did. My only wish was for her to be happy and I wished them *mazel tov*, congratulations. Emil had never married before, so I am sure it was not easy for him to take on a new family.

My mother's marriage brought some stability into her life, but it did not affect me. Although Emil did express his opinions, he did not interfere with mine. Emil didn't try to be my father; he wanted just to be Ibi's husband. There was no reason for our paths to cross, and instinctually, I was unobtrusive when it came to their relationship.

In 1960, our family expanded when my mother's younger sister, Elizabeth, immigrated to Canada with her husband, Frank, and their son, Tomi. Along with Aranka, Jenö and Marianna, this was the extent of our family. Except for my grandparents, we had no other close relatives. During this period, we received our citizenship papers and became true Canadians.

~

As soon as I turned eighteen, I obtained my Red Cross Swimming Instructors' Certificate and Royal Lifesaving Society Bronze Cross, and I got a part-time job as a swimming instructor. One of my students was a pretty fourteen-year-old girl named Judy, who looked older than her age. I didn't know at the time that she was the daughter of two of Emil's friends.

I attended a friend's bar mitzvah with my steady girlfriend, Sarah, where Judy was also a guest, along with her parents. As Sarah and I walked through the door, Judy shouted over the loud music, "Andy, what are you doing here? I almost didn't recognize you with your clothes on." Naturally that was the split second when the music stopped. Fortunately, most people knew that I was a swimming instructor, and my answer helped ease Judy's deep embarrassment. I told her that my bathing suit was in the car, since I never went anywhere without it.

Sarah and I broke up very shortly afterwards, but not because of that incident. Although I was on my way to becoming a Canadian, I still had a lot of the old country in me. I was also being introduced to some Jewish customs and culture, which can be quite different from the Jewish religion. Sarah's parents, both Holocaust survivors, were from Poland. Since they had come to Canada soon after the war, I considered them Canadian, especially Sarah, who was born in Canada and had no accent.

For Sarah's eighteenth birthday, I gave her an expensive white-gold watch to show her my feelings for her. Her parents wanted to know if it was an engagement present. At first, I did not understand their question. When it was repeated, I said no, it was a birthday gift. My response brought about an interesting result: Sarah became engaged three months after her eighteenth birthday to someone else.

Tradition and custom among some Jewish families dictated that a young woman be married before she turned twenty. This custom, of which I had no knowledge at the time, was practised far more among

Polish Jews than Hungarian Jews. I, however, simply wasn't ready for marriage.

Although I was definitely not heartbroken, simply a bit perplexed and sad, my stepfather, Emil, felt that he should try to cheer me up. He told me that Sarah was not for me since she was short, wore glasses and was Polish. His last concern was the most puzzling. I never asked him to elaborate. Years later I found out that Hungarian Jews were generally a lot more assimilated into their new country's culture and removed from the old traditions than Polish Jews were. Consequently, Hungarian Jews and Polish Jews – two branches from the same family tree – tended not to mix.

Young and Carefree

I couldn't imagine not working for a living, and I certainly enjoyed the fruits of my labour. I continued to live at home and pay my share of the expenses, which left me with a fair amount of disposable income. I used it to enjoy all the benefits this country could offer. I was a modern Canadian citizen.

In June 1961, when graduation rolled around, I faced the dreaded question, What are you going to be? It was not an easy question to answer. One thing became obvious: I was not going to university. Although my mother and Emil would have helped me financially, I wasn't a great student; I did not have the discipline necessary to study. I told my mother that to study you don't need brains, you need ass, meaning you just need to sit down and take the time to study. After more than forty years, I still stand by this statement. Over the years, I have met people with little formal education who possessed great intellect. Conversely, I have also encountered some highly educated intellectual lightweights, especially among politicians.

By 1961, the employment rate was decreasing, so choosing a career was more difficult. At Central Tech, I had been exposed to drafting and shop work. By then, I knew that engineering was not my forte. I wanted to enter the field of photography. Being young and naïve, I accepted a job with a printing company as an apprentice photoengraver, believing it had to do with photography. As it turned out, it was a specialized field in its dying days. Technology was already replacing the old masters. It was not a wise career choice.

Fortunately, I received a response to an application I had sent in previously and was invited for an interview with John T. Hepburn Limited, a large manufacturer of structural steel components for bridges, office buildings and such. On the strength of having attended Central Tech and my exposure to drafting, I was accepted as an apprentice structural steel detailer with the goal of becoming a draftsman. I signed a three-year apprenticeship contract, which my mother co-signed, since I was still a minor. During the three years, I was to attend the Provincial Institute of Trades (which later became George Brown College) for a three-month basic and a three-month advanced course in structural steel theory.

As the new apprentice, I was also the gofer. It was my job to take everybody's orders for the coffee breaks, make deliveries and just generally be useful. Peter, the chief draftsman at Hepburn who spoke with a heavy Scottish brogue, did not like coffee or tea and ordered a Coke. When I asked him what size, he got very upset with me for asking such a stupid question. "The darned thing only comes in one size!" When I insisted that Coca Cola came in various sizes, he responded, "No, no, no! Not Coke. Cocoa! Hot chocolate in your language." (He meant Canadian English.) I took Peter's comment as a great compliment that by then I was truly Canadian. "What's the matter with you," he said, "don't you speak the Queen's English?" Not until then I didn't. For years to come, some people thought my accent was Scottish. I was happy to inform them that it was Hungarian.

Structural steel detailing was an interesting job with good career opportunities. However, within a year, I knew that I did not like it. I wanted to quit, but my mother urged me to get my certificate. She reminded me that I had to finish whatever I started. Since I didn't want to disappoint my mother, I completed the apprenticeship. Although I did not distinguish myself with high marks, I passed all the courses and obtained my draftsman's certificate.

At that time, I still didn't know what I wanted to do career-wise, only what I did not want to do. In addition, my mother had taught me to behave honourably. Since the good people at Hepburn had invested their time and money in me, I stayed a little over a year with them as a draftsman before going to work for a competitor. In total, I spent seven years behind the drafting table.

All my friends were in the same position as I was – working at a full-time job, living at home, owning their own car, going to the same parties, dating from the same group of girls. We were living the good life. During this time, I bought my first brand new car, a 1962 Ford Falcon. My friends and I took camping trips with that car all over Ontario: to Jackson's Point on Lake Simcoe, Bigwin Island in the Muskokas and Algonquin Provincial Park. In the winter, we drove to Blue Mountain in Collingwood and even farther north to ski. We were all in the same boat, both figuratively and literally, when we went water skiing in the summer. We were young and carefree.

~

In December 1962, I took a two-week trip to Europe, planning on hostelling, which was tailor-made for a social creature like me. I travelled alone only between cities. While I was travelling on a train from Zurich, Switzerland, to Vienna, Austria, the passports of all my fellow travellers were very closely scrutinized. When the conductor saw my Canadian passport, he just said "Danke," thank you, and walked past me. I experienced this great respect for Canada many more times in my future travels.

I spent one week in the Austrian Alps with a group of other adventurers I had met at the hostel. I decided to spend the second week visiting my grandparents in Budapest, which was only three hours away. There were a few technical difficulties connected with that decision. In those days, it was impossible to go behind the Iron Curtain without a visa and be assured of getting back out.

Although I was a Canadian citizen, I was a naturalized citizen with dual citizenship. I had unofficially renounced my Hungarian citizenship, but Hungary had never relinquished its claim on me – I was still eligible for the military draft in Hungary. Quite unexpectedly, the question of my citizenship came up at the Hungarian embassy when I applied for a visa. When I was asked about my citizenship, I very proudly declared that I was Canadian and showed my passport as confirmation. My Canadian passport showed Budapest as my place of birth. I was told that since I had been born in Hungary, I would have to fill in my visa application as a Hungarian citizen. I told the official that I would not do that under any circumstances, because I had never been a citizen of Hungary. The official wanted me to explain.

For me it was an easy explanation: My father had been deported from Hungary. He had been forced into a labour camp because he was a Jew and not a Hungarian. How could the son of a non-Hungarian become a citizen? I asked. I knew that I was being a bigmouth, but I felt that if they didn't want me in Hungary as a citizen of a free country like Canada, then I wouldn't get the visa and would simply not go to Hungary. Fortunately, the official, an older man, gave me my visa.

I called my mother, but not until I was in Hungary, since I didn't wish to worry her. She told me later that if I hadn't wanted to worry her, then I shouldn't have gone to Hungary at all. I couldn't phone ahead to my grandparents because they didn't have a phone, and my poor grandmother nearly had a heart attack from the shock of seeing me. My visit consisted of four days of euphoria for all of us. In addition to my beloved grandparents, I had the opportunity to see all my old friends and some of my old classmates, who introduced me to the nightlife of Budapest.

My grandparents and I went to my father's gravesite, where my grandfather read the prayers in Hebrew, reciting the Kaddish. This was the first time I had heard anything related to religion coming from my grandfather, and I found out that he was quite learned in Judaism. The gravesite is not where my father's remains are actually buried; we don't know where his remains are. Since his body was never found, he never received a proper burial. The cemetery contains row upon row of markers for some of the hundreds of thousands of Jews from Hungary who were murdered in the Holocaust.

I was fortunate enough to see my beloved grandparents again in 1963, much sooner than I expected. My mother and Emil decided to have my grandparents celebrate their fiftieth anniversary with us in Toronto. In those days, the Iron Curtain was still tightly shut, and family visits were very rare. Having never met my grandparents, Emil had no ties to them, yet he and my mother signed a sponsorship guarantee in order for my grandparents to be allowed into Canada.

From the day we picked up my grandparents at the airport until the day they left, the visit entailed one delightful experience after another. The anniversary celebration itself was a surprise for my grandparents. My two aunts were there with their families, making eleven of us altogether. It was exactly eighteen years after the Holocaust.

Growing Up

As all my friends and I approached adulthood, the numbers in our large circle started to dwindle. Some got married, some moved away and others just drifted apart. We were all settling down. My friend Julius was the first of our group to get married. I was the best man at his wedding, after which I never saw him again. Peter was next; he was going to invite me to his new apartment when he had finished unpacking. That was over thirty years ago. I guess he had a lot of boxes to unpack. I kept in touch with Mike, but it became a long-distance friendship when he moved to Montreal. Mike and I had been friends from kindergarten and all through public school. We had both left Hungary at the same time. Like my mother, his mother, a widow, had remarried.

In 1967, I got a three-month assignment in Montreal as a steel draftsman. I moved in with Mike and his wife, Erna, for that period. We had some great times during those three months. My stay co-incided with the Canadian Centennial – the celebration of the one-hundredth anniversary of Canada's Confederation – and Montreal hosted a world fair called Expo '67. It was Canada's showcase for the world. An entire island had been built in the St. Lawrence River as the site, and the world was beating a path to Canada's doorstep.

For those three months, I practically lived at Expo. Sometimes I went there straight from work. Mike and Erna introduced me to some of their friends, and we did a lot together. It was almost like the good old days in Toronto. Those heady days in Montreal came to an end when my contract was up. Expo '67 and our booming economy both came to a sudden halt. Upon my return to Toronto, I had a great deal of difficulty finding a job.

However, it was because I lost my job that I found Magdi. Her name was Magdalene, but everybody called her Maggie – except me. I had first met Magdi when she was only sixteen. She lived on a small farm with her parents and sister in Grassie, Ontario, about one hundred kilometres from Toronto. Her father and Emil were *landsmen*, born in the same town, and Emil wanted to introduce his new family to the Vadnai family. In the Niagara Escarpment area, a number of Hungarian Jewish families operated different kinds of farms, and Magdi's parents owned a dairy farm. That was the first time I met Magdi. I didn't see her again until 1968, when I blundered into the bank where she was working in Toronto.

After Expo '67, jobs were scarce. I worked at a few jobs, including selling insurance and driving a taxi, before I landed a job at the City of Toronto's Works Department. The job was supposedly drafting, but not in my field of expertise. There were fifty-two people in the department, despite the fact that we didn't have enough work for two.

The Works Department was located in City Hall. Inside the building was a small branch of a bank, where all City Hall employees did their banking. I went there to cash my first paycheque. Magdi, now a bank teller, recognized me instantly, but I didn't recognize her or make any connection with her name, which was on her nameplate for all to see. She didn't say anything at the time about recognizing me. On my second visit, the Hungarian name on a nameplate intrigued me, and I struck up a polite conversation – with the wrong girl! Magdi was on her lunch break, and the teller replacing her had not changed the nameplate on the counter.

The third time, all the stars were aligned. I still did not connect Magdi with my visit to her home some years ago. But at least I realized that the girl with the Hungarian name was not her colleague.

The bank was a very busy place during lunchtime, not the proper place for idle chit-chat. I wanted to tell her about my confusion and wanted to know if she could speak Hungarian. She told me that yes, she could speak Hungarian, that we had already spoken before and that I should please not hold up the people behind me. I searched my meagre memory bank, but I could not recall her at all.

During the afternoon coffee break, I went back to the bank to ask for some more information. She was not gushing with enthusiasm, but she was courteous and solved the great mystery for me. This young lady intrigued me. I asked her when she usually went to lunch and where she went to eat. She told me that she took very little time for lunch because the bank was too busy.

It wasn't a definite rejection, but it also wasn't an acceptance. I hate ambiguity, so I just persisted until I got Magdi to agree to have lunch with me. It took only two days. So, we had our first date some five years after our first meeting. We ate sandwiches at the fountain in front of City Hall. It was June 1968, just a few weeks before my twenty-sixth birthday.

I still lived at home, and I drove to work every day with my mother, who was also working downtown, at the Bank of Montreal head office on King Street, close to City Hall. One day, while driving to work, I noticed Magdi waiting for the bus. We stopped for her, and from then on I drove her to work every day together with my mother.

We never really had a proper date. We were always accompanied either by my mother or Magdi's sister, Margaret. The two young women lived together in an apartment, and every weekend they drove out to the farm to be with their parents. Magdi and I did not go out to movies or restaurants or any of the usual places that young people go during a courtship. We only drove to work together in the morning and, in fact, there was very little opportunity to date. By then, I definitely liked her. So did my mother, who was getting to know Magdi at the same time as I was. It was an unusual situation. Since Magdi was the daughter of Emil's friend, Emil liked her as well.

For my birthday, Magdi gave me a tie in appreciation for the rides to work. After that, I went over to Magdi and Margaret's apartment a couple of times a week, and we got to know each other better, but we still hadn't had a proper date.

My car was beginning to fall apart, so I bought a brand new 1968 Plymouth with a big V8 engine. One of the first trips with the new car was a visit to Magdi's parents on the farm, along with her sister, Margaret. Unbeknownst to me, their father, Miklós, was a practitioner of the old ways in more ways than one. For one, he was a Kabbalist, very learned in Jewish mysticism. He even conducted some of the High Holiday services for their small Jewish farming community in Lincoln County, Ontario. What I also didn't know was that, just like Sarah's parents, Magdi's father had previously tried to arrange an early marriage for his daughter. However, Magdi, unlike Sarah, did not go along with her father's wishes. She wasn't defiant; she was independent.

Magdi's family were also Holocaust survivors; her mother, Ilonka, had been in Auschwitz and was one of the victims of the horrendous scientific experiments of Dr. Mengele, also known as the "Angel of Death." Her father escaped from his forced labour battalion and joined the Soviet partisans to fight the Germans. During the Holocaust, his entire first family, including two daughters from his first marriage, perished in the gas chambers.

I am convinced that, although Magdi was born after the Holocaust, she was a victim of that period. She was born in 1946, when her mother was still weak from the effects of starvation and the torture she had been subjected to. Magdi's magnificent spirit and thirst for knowledge were slowed by her various illnesses – arthritis, fibromyalgia, migraines. I believe that her ailments were due to her mother's previous sufferings and that her mother's illnesses were passed on to Magdi.

Magdi's spirit showed itself very early in our relationship. Her twenty-second birthday was in September, and my gift to her was a diamond engagement ring. I wanted to surprise her, but I was the one who was surprised. She said no! I was at a stage in my life when I still didn't know what I was going to do career-wise, but I could certainly recognize a "diamond" in front of my nose when it came to having a partner for life. I usually don't give up easily on anything, and I knew this young lady was special. In spite of the short duration of our relationship, I recognized a lot of the basic ingredients needed for a successful marriage. In addition to my persevering nature, I had a secret ally in Magdi's father, Miklós, although I didn't know it at the time. As a result of all the hardships he had endured, including the hard life at the farm, Miklós was already in poor health from a previous heart attack.

In his youth, Miklós had studied under a famous Kabbalist, Rabbi Yeshayah Steiner, known in local circles as a *tzaddik,* an extremely righteous man. One of the most profound events in Miklós's life was when Rabbi Steiner foretold the exact time of his own impending death. Miklós also had certain qualities of prescience: he knew he didn't have much longer to live. When Magdi refused my proposal, Miklós's health was rapidly deteriorating. He expressed his fervent wish to live long enough to see both his daughters marry "nice Jewish boys."

When Magdi turned me down, she didn't say, "I never want to see you again," and I definitely wanted to see her again. The following day, I showed up as if nothing had happened and asked her to go for a ride with me. My shiny new car still needed breaking in, so we drove the hundred kilometres to her parents' house. When we got there, I asked Miklós for his permission to marry his daughter. His instant reply was yes. Magdi asked if she had any say in the matter. In unison, Miklós and I said no. Magdi did not put up that much of a fight, for she had mixed feelings. She had had a crush on me when she first met me, and remembered me as tall, good-looking and blue-eyed. I wasn't tall; she was just shorter at the time. When we met again at City Hall years later, she'd grown taller, so now we were about the same height.

She wasn't ready to marry someone that she couldn't look up to, literally. Hard as I tried to convince her that physical appearance was not important, I couldn't sell her on the idea until the day of our wedding. Because she never wanted to appear taller than me, she never wore high-heeled shoes.

When my parents visited the farm a week after my proposal, the engagement became official. After our engagement, Magdi, her sister, Margaret, and I went to the farm every weekend, returning to Toronto Sunday evenings. My family definitely started to grow. Magdi's maternal uncle, also named Miklós, lived on the next farm with his wife, Margit, and their son, Steve. There were about thirty Jewish farming families living in this area at the time, and they were all invited to our wedding.

We arranged and paid for our own wedding. Magdi's parents were financially strapped, and I couldn't expect my parents to carry the expense. Magdi wanted a big wedding, which was not an issue for us. We could afford it, since we were both working. The wedding took place three months after the engagement, on December 15, 1968, in Hamilton, the closest city to the farm. Miklós did not feel up to travelling, and Hamilton was only sixty-five kilometres from Toronto. The whole "shtetl" was there, and we followed all the Jewish traditions. Magdi was the first child from the small Jewish farming community to be married.

It was at the wedding that I was able to settle the height issue once and for all. We had never danced with each other before. In fact, neither of us even knew if the other could dance. It turned out that we both knew the steps to every dance, be it the cha-cha, tango, rumba or waltz and, of course, rock and roll. Magdi had learned how to dance from her father. We were in perfect harmony, as if we had rehearsed.

On our wedding day, Magdi declared that since I was such a good dancer, she knew that I had potential. Our heights were never an issue from that day on. I always tried to live up to my potential in everything, including being a good husband and father.

The Quest Continues

I believe that three ingredients are needed for a successful life: a good family life; good spiritual, mental and physical health; and an occupation that one enjoys. I was on my way to obtaining a good family life, and I now had a partner to share it with.

Magdi's sister, Margaret, moved in with a girlfriend downtown, and I moved into Magdi's furnished apartment. I only had to bring my clothes and good intentions. We continued to visit Magdi's parents every weekend, leaving straight from work on Fridays. This became very important to all of us, because we celebrated the arrival of Shabbat in the traditional manner. We had family meals, and her father read the traditional prayers.

Ilonka started cooking for the Shabbat meals days ahead. She could hardly wait for Friday. These Shabbat dinners exposed me to Jewish traditions I hadn't grown up with. Although my stepfather, Emil, an observant Jew, celebrated Shabbat in a similar manner and went to synagogue every Saturday, he had never demanded my participation. With the exception of the High Holidays, I had not participated in any Jewish rituals, but I wanted to be a part of Magdi's family.

Magdi's parents grew to like me. Miklós told me a lot of fascinating stories, both personal and religious. For Ilonka, I was the perfect guest: I ate everything put in front of me, sometimes second helpings (especially of her *kuglóf*). My early training by my grandmother kicked in: I never forgot to compliment Ilonka. Magdi got along with my parents equally well, but we spent much more time with her parents.

Going to her parents' farm every weekend introduced me to the family's neighbours, friends and some honest-to-goodness farm work. We went out to the farm as much as we could, but we soon became busy with our new lifestyle. Whenever we went to the farm, though, I always learned something, including the story behind the Jewish farming community of Beamsville, Ontario, which Grassie was part of, being only fifteen kilometres away.

People often ask me, Are there really Jewish farmers? The question never fails to surprise me. Why not? In fact, could Israel exist if Jews didn't know how to work the land? Did we not get instruction in the Bible about how to leave the land fallow every seven years? Didn't the early pioneers of Israel turn the desert into orchards by knowing how to work the land?

Baron Maurice de Hirsch founded the Jewish Colonization Association in 1891 to encourage Jews to form agricultural communities, a sort of "returning to the land" in the biblical sense, in my opinion. When Magdi's parents arrived in Canada in March 1957, a subsidiary of the foundation was still in existence as the Jewish Agricultural Society. A subsidized loan was available to help in the purchase of a farm, and after five years, a clear title of ownership was obtained. About forty Jewish families, mostly from Hungary, took up the offer and settled in Lincoln Township.

Most of the families took up fruit farming. Magdi's parents, however, went into dairy farming, which is one of the most demanding types of farming. The cattle have to be milked and fed seven days a week. The barn has to be cleaned of manure regularly. The cattle feed has to be either produced or bought, the equipment repaired and a myriad of other problems taken care of on a daily basis. But Miklós loved it. He never travelled far from the farm. In fact, he never even visited either of his daughters' homes.

During the fall of 1969, Miklós suffered a heart attack, and Magdi and I moved out to the farm temporarily to help with the work. Miklós had rented a property nearby, where he was growing feed for the cattle. It was harvest time and I drove the tractor, which had the baling machine attached to it.

Through my wife and in-laws, I continued to be exposed to Judaism. In typical fashion, the small Hungarian-Jewish community wanted to have their own cultural centre. They purchased a former one-room schoolhouse to be used as a combination recreation centre and synagogue. The centre was the location of the High Holiday services, conducted by Miklós. I had never attended an Orthodox service before, where men and women sit separately, something Miklós explained to me before the services. I was also prohibited from taking photos or movies during the services, but I did not heed this request. As a result, we have some beautiful memories captured on film of Miklós leading the congregation in prayer. Unfortunately, this was before video-recording cameras had sound, and Miklós had a magnificent voice. He read from our prayer book in Hebrew, but the commentary and explanations were in Hungarian. The High Holiday services that I had previously attended with Emil and my mother had been conducted in Hebrew and Yiddish, a language I never knew existed before I came to Canada.

~

I had obtained my cab driver's licence in 1966 and driven part-time for a while, but I hadn't had the intention of making it permanent. After marrying Magdi, I started to drive part-time again. I liked driving a taxi. I am a people person, outgoing and easy to engage in conversation. I could make enough money driving a taxi on the weekend to pay for our entertainment expenses, which meant we could use our salaries to pay off our debts connected with the wedding.

During a drive up north to spend a long weekend in Muskoka, Magdi and I discussed my dissatisfaction with drafting and my desire to have my own business. Magdi suggested we buy a taxi. I thought that it was such a great idea that I wanted to turn around and start working on it right away. She had to hold on to the wheel to stop me from doing so.

Buying a taxi definitely required work. The value of a taxi plate was $15,000, which was a lot of money in those days. Between the two of us, we had $500 to our names. When Magdi found out the cost of a taxicab, she tried to convince me to forget the idea, but it was too late; I was already hooked. We borrowed the money from seven different people. My mother and stepfather loaned us all their savings and in November 1969, I became the proud owner of Metropolitan Toronto taxicab 855. My objective was to pay off taxicab 855 quickly, and it took us only one year to pay back everybody in full. The significance of the number 855, which was assigned to me by my great future nemesis, the Metropolitan Toronto Licensing Commission, was pointed out to me by Shirley, one of our neighbours. She said that I would always be lucky with that number since the numerals in 855 add up to eighteen, which signifies good luck in Judaism. To this day, some people refer to me as Andy 855.

When we first bought taxicab 855, our family car, the 1968 Plymouth, became part of the deal. We gave it to the vendor as part of the $15,000 purchase price. Taxi 855, a 1968 Ford, became our family car when I wasn't working in it. This was the common practice among one-cab owners/drivers. Magdi used 855 to go shopping for groceries on the weekends.

It was a strange coincidence that both Magdi and my mother worked for banks. In those days, almost all bank supervisors were men; very few women had management positions. Both Magdi and my mother experienced difficulties in the workplace. Magdi did her boss's work; he was a man who drank his lunch. She also stayed behind many times to do extra work without any compensation. My mother was subjected to some workplace harassment from her fellow workers, which her supervisor turned a blind eye to. Their situations were always on my mind and affected me profoundly.

Although I knew that Magdi was being treated unfairly at the bank, it would be a while before we could deal with those problems, since I was working fourteen-hour days. I assured Magdi's parents by invoking a Hungarian saying, which roughly translates as "While I am able to work, I will always be a good provider and Magdi will not be lacking."

I was making a good living, so in the fall of 1970, we decided to take a trip to Hungary for four weeks. A few weeks before we left for Hungary, we attended the wedding of Magdi's sister, Margaret. Margaret married Morton (Morty), who was Canadian born, hailing from Montreal. In Hungary, Magdi met my grandparents, and it was love at first sight. We also visited Magdi's place of birth, Vadna, where her family had changed its name from Weiss to Vadnai. Magdi met many of my childhood friends, and we had a great time.

One week after we got back from our trip, on August 25, 1970, Miklós suffered a fatal heart attack. I was the last person to talk to him, and I was holding his hand when he died. He was only sixty-two. God had granted him his wish, to live long enough to see both his daughters married to nice Jewish boys. Miklós's death devastated all of us. Ilonka couldn't possibly run the farm by herself. The animals had to be looked after even during the shiva, the traditional seven-day period of mourning for Jewish people. It was also harvest time again. Fortunately, some of the neighbours and their children were able to help. However, school was starting soon, and permanent hired help was expensive and very difficult to secure. The farm was not a profit-making business; it just provided a living. After the shiva, Ilonka decided to sell the farm.

Ilonka moved to Toronto, and I went back to my regular fourteen-hour workdays. Magdi and I moved to a nicer apartment and settled into a routine. We were expecting our first child. Both future grandmothers were happy. By coincidence, my mother and Ilonka were exactly the same age. By an equally strange coincidence, having survived the Holocaust, one was fated to be alone in her youth and the other in her golden years. No matter how we pleaded with Ilonka, she was not willing to meet anybody.

Ilonka was really looking forward to being a grandmother. After David was born on May 23, 1971, she became our permanent babysitter, since she lived just across the street from our apartment. My mother and Emil came to our apartment frequently to see their grandson, but Ilonka spent much more time with David. My mother was still working at the time.

The apartment where we lived was being converted into a condominium, and the owner wanted to make it an adults-only building. As a result, we decided to buy a house instead of looking for another apartment. Magdi was back at work, so the location of the home had to be carefully chosen. No matter how we tried, we could not find anything affordable close to where we wanted to live. We ended up in a part of the city that was a good neighbourhood but on the cheaper side of the street. It was located right next to Highway 401 near Bayview Avenue. It had two advantages: a nursery school nearby and a branch of the bank that Magdi could walk to. Due to my constant concern for Magdi's welfare at work, she eventually agreed to quit the bank and become a stay-at-home mother and wife. Fortunately, I was earning sufficient income by this time to support our family.

Emil very generously offered to give us the down payment for a more expensive house, but Magdi and I felt we could not accept it. However, I made Emil a proposal of my own: to go into partnership to buy a second cab together. We did just that. By 1972, I was a homeowner, a father and the owner of one and a half cabs. Life in Canada was good.

Behind the Wheel

"The taxi business is the easiest business to get into and the hardest to get out of." I had no idea how right my dispatcher was when I first heard him say this in 1969. I spent eleven years behind the wheel of a taxi. During that time, I had three physical confrontations, with one win, one loss and one draw. Each fight started the moment I hit back. One fight wasn't even my fight when it started. It was a confrontation between Arnie, my new friend from the taxi business, and the dispatcher. I only stepped in to back up Arnie and to stop the argument from escalating. When I tried to intervene, the dispatcher turned on me: "You f***ing little DP! I am going to make you sorry for not only the day you joined Co-op Taxi, but for the day you were born. From now on, I won't even give you the orders that you deserve."

In the taxi business, where swear words are considered terms of endearment, I felt that "DP," the abbreviation for "displaced person," was an insult that went beyond the normal shop talk. It refers to any person driven from their homeland, but in this case, he really meant me, as a Jew who had come to Canada after the war. I was a landed immigrant and by this time a very proud Canadian citizen. Sadly, the man was abusing his position as a dispatcher by giving certain cab drivers the more lucrative fares. Even more sadly, he was a Jew himself.

I came from a neighbourhood where I had witnessed my share of fights. A Russian had pointed a gun at me, and I had spent time in jail with my mother. But up until that moment, I had never faced injustice in such a raw, vicious and personal manner. When the dispatcher threatened me, he also threatened my livelihood and my family.

The taxi business seemed to have a lot of corrupt practices in those days, both within the brokerages and at the Licensing Commission, which was the industry regulator. The dispatcher received payments from some cab drivers to give them preferential treatment. Many other dispatchers did the same thing. They decided who got the thirty-dollar run and who got the three-dollar run. I didn't pay off anybody, and neither did Arnie. As a result, we made less money than some other drivers.

In those days, the average income for a cabby was about fifty dollars a day. We found out that certain drivers averaged one hundred and fifty a day. I was making my living on the leftovers and from picking up passengers on the street. To be told that I wouldn't get any orders, not even what my monthly dispatch fee entitled me to, was too much for me. I got angry.

Many before me had gone to Lou Friedman, the manager of Co-op Cabs, with complaints about favouritism. Uncle Lou, as everyone called him, was not involved with the favouritism personally, but he knew what was going on. He was a bachelor who considered his dispatchers to be his children. Anybody who dared to accuse his precious dispatchers was told, "If you can't prove your accusation, I will personally throw you out of the company." And he did fire several cabbies.

When Lou brushed off my concern about his dispatcher's threat against me, I accused him of being in on the take. He wasn't and I knew that, but I figured it would be more of an even fight if he lost his cool. He hit the roof, and then he went into his spiel. I was ready for him; I had heard all about this speech from the others. I told Lou that I was a shareholder in this company and that I could not be thrown out by him alone. Even if I were thrown out, I would carry on my fight against him and Co-op. Lou was a bully, but I had dealt with bullies before.

When bullying didn't work, Lou challenged me to dispatch. He wanted to show me how difficult dispatching was. To my knowledge, nobody had ever taken Lou up on his challenge besides me. I know that after I did it, he never made that offer to anybody ever again. I stood my ground and dispatched for forty minutes before the dispatcher who had threatened me relieved me.

All my life, I had heard my mother say how she detested injustice. When injustice was in front of me, I had to do something about it. The investigation into my charges took a year and a half to complete. To prove my allegation, I collated the times and destinations of the cab drivers' orders, which were kept on record. I was a threat to both recipients and perpetrators of the bribes, since they stood to lose big money. During this time, my car was vandalized, and I was warned to watch my back. Even Lou was concerned (he was a decent man). Eventually it was confirmed that some of the dispatchers were accepting payments in return for preferential treatment, and the Board of Directors ordered Lou to fire my dispatcher as well as two other dispatchers.

In the end, Lou and I became friends and the best of enemies at the same time. Lou even made me the head of the disciplinary committee. In time, I became a member of the Board of Directors, recording secretary and vice-president of Co-op Cabs.

The taxi business attracted a lot of different kinds of people from different backgrounds. Before the taxi business seeped into our blood, we had all done something else, so we all had stories. We even had a favourite hangout to exchange these stories – the cafeteria at a hotel called the Inn on the Park.

As cab drivers, we were allowed to eat in the staff cafeteria, where we enjoyed some pretty good dinners at very low prices. Even though we were supposed to just eat and go back to work, we talked shop. We had some very lively discussions there. Some people liked to discuss the destinations of their runs and how much was showing on the meter. I liked to tell human-interest stories, especially if they were funny. Since we were dealing with the public, we all had many anecdotes. Sadly, taxi driving also had dangers – the murder of a fellow cabbie affected me deeply, and I wrote the following article in *Taxi News*.

PEACE

The minister had just finished his sermon and eulogy. He asked us to turn to each other, shake hands and say "Peace." What a beautiful, wonderful word! How good it made me feel! How glad I was to be amongst men of good will!

Then the casket was moved along the aisle, and the procession started to follow. That is when I met him for the first time: Robert Nankoo, a fellow human being, a young man, a father, a husband, a fallen brother, a member of our taxi fraternity.

I saw his widow with her children. One was clinging to her waist, the other in her arms. My eyes swelled and I couldn't hold back any longer. I shed a tear for him, for her, for her children, for humanity … for peace.

We also had our opinions on politics, especially Co-op and Licensing Commission politics. The internal wars at Co-op subsided somewhat. The blatant favouritism, cheating and payola had decreased but not stopped completely. We were dealing with taxi people, a most inventive and determined bunch of people.

A year after my investigation, Lou Friedman passed away. His death left Co-op Cabs in great turmoil, without a general manager. As vice-president of Co-op, I was one of three people in charge of finding a replacement. We were also responsible for running the company. I was all of thirty-six, and certainly naïve. Workplace politics was something with which I was totally unfamiliar. I was quickly jolted out of my naïveté. My friend Joe Tripodi – president of Co-op at the time – the company auditor and I decided that the manager of fleet operation, who was already the assistant general manager, was the right man to take Lou's place as general manager.

Our search committee made a huge mistake in not placing any conditions or proper controls on our new general manager. In no time at all, he consolidated his control over the company. In those days, the general manager was allowed to be a board director, which gave him additional, and at times extraordinary, powers. Because of the new general manager, I was not there to see this unhealthy transformation personally.

I was faced with some weighty problems that needed careful deliberation. The new general manager, it seems, unwittingly launched me on my third career. When the fleet manager was promoted to general manager, his previous position of assistant general manager became vacant. I never discussed my desire to fill the job with him or anyone else. At one of the regular board meetings, I simply came right out and stated that I wanted the job and that I was the right person for it. The new general manager banged his hand on the table and said in no uncertain terms (I believe he used the phrase "over my dead body") that he neither needed nor wanted an assistant. I was insulted and devastated at being denied this job. I was also ready to stop driving a cab. Taxi driving is certainly not the easiest job in the world.

Two Families

Work was just the necessary backdrop for my family life. Magdi and I were adjusting to being parents. The birth of our son in 1971 diminished our social life but enhanced our family life. Magdi and I developed a wonderful friendship with her childhood friend Judy and Judy's husband, Ernie. Our children were similar in age, and our two families spent a lot of time together. A number of times we rented a cottage for the whole summer. The women stayed there with the kids while Ernie and I drove up on the weekends. Our two families also rented a recreational vehicle, which we drove to Florida during the winter break. We often celebrated birthday parties for the kids and our family members together. We were growing into our family roles as parents.

In the mid-seventies, my friend Arnie Partnoy introduced me to B'nai Brith, and I joined Leonard Mayzel Ontario Lodge, which was one of the largest in Toronto. At this point, I was beginning to close the gaps in my Jewish identity, although I was hardly aware of it at the time. B'nai Brith was a large organization dedicated to community service, with the simple motto "People Helping People." I found new friends and new projects, but most importantly, a way to help others.

At the first lodge meeting I attended, I saw and heard Alvin Abram, who later became the president of our lodge. Alvin was also an instigator and a kindred spirit, and I liked him from the moment I heard him argue. At the time, he was the editor of our award-winning lodge bulletin, *The Observer*. Alvin welcomed my and my mother's articles for *The Observer*.

Members of B'nai Brith call one another brothers and sisters, and indeed my lodge members became like a second family to me. Magdi and I, and later our son, David, had a very active life in B'nai Brith. David bowled with me every Thursday night, and he was the captain of our lodge's team. We also made many new friends and participated in numerous activities, both social and community-oriented. We went on picnics with groups of 350 or more. We went to conventions, bowling tournaments and dinners. We took children with disabilities on outings, helped with bingo games and charity casinos, and sold raffle tickets. We participated in Red Cross blood donor clinics, organized car pools to drive seniors to appointments and distributed food baskets to those less fortunate. We received back in warm smiles just as much as we gave.

Every year, B'nai Brith lodges hold an annual convention. Magdi and I attended our first-ever convention in 1977 at the Nevele Grand Hotel in the Catskill Mountains in New York State. It was one of the famous "Borscht Belt" hotels, a term for summer resorts in upstate New York that were popular with Jewish families from the 1920s to 1970s. We all had a wonderful time there, filled with friendship and camaraderie. We are also certain that our daughter, Kati, is a Nevele baby, and we named all delegates from our lodge godparents to her. Our family was definitely expanding!

The birth of our daughter, Kati, whose Hebrew name is Golde bat Hillel, on February 12, 1978, found us in a very happy place in our lives. We had moved to a bigger home and purchased our third taxi. Reflecting on those times, I know how fortunate I was to have been blessed with a loving and caring family. Having other outlets, like my swimming and B'nai Brith activities, provided much-needed relief.

Magdi helped resolve my dilemma with my career at Co-op by once again pointing me in the right direction for a career change. Although she didn't know what was involved, she thought that my becoming a real estate agent might be a good idea. This idea had actually come from Magdi's best friend from high school, Janice, and her husband, Leo Leplante, who lived in Niagara Falls. They had both become real estate agents and opened up their own company.

For a number of years, whenever we got together, they had tried to encourage us to move down to Niagara Falls and me to get my real estate licence. Leo felt that I would make a good salesperson. I had never paid too much attention. We had our family and our friends in Toronto. I had no intention then of selling the cabs or moving away.

Magdi's idea was not to move but to practise real estate in Toronto. As before, I was in charge of working out the details. To obtain a real estate licence in 1980 required the completion of a three-week course and a passing grade of 75 per cent. I graduated from the course in August 1980, having initially failed one class and barely passing it the second time. My graduation was strictly the result of my mother's patience and devotion.

In those days, we had to memorize twenty-two clauses that were part of a standard real estate offer. These clauses had to be written out from memory during the final exam. Everybody in my family is blessed with a great memory, except me. Magdi, who had a near photographic memory, couldn't understand my difficulty with such an easy task. Later on, when Magdi took the real estate exam, she got 98 per cent. Interestingly, she proved the point of our instructor, who told us that most people who get a high mark do not last in the business, while people like me, who struggle through the course, do very well.

Memorization work was torture for me. My mother offered to help me memorize the realty clauses and spent many days doing so. It was exactly what she'd done for me when I was in grade school and struggling to memorize the multiplication tables. I do have a good ability to grasp, recognize and analyze issues. In many of the sales training courses that I took during my real estate career, the underlying issue was how to make a sale – you recognize a client's "needs and wants" factors, you formulate a plan and you execute the plan.

The taxi and real estate businesses had similarities, particularly the need to understand and, even more importantly, like people. I've always been an outgoing, enthusiastic person who understands and enjoys being with people. In addition, my goal-setting ability, which I developed from competitive swimming, and my knowledge of Toronto neighbourhoods, which I gained from driving taxis, were also a great help with my real estate career. The real estate business went through a number of boom and bust cycles, but I stayed with it. At one point, Emil and I sold a fourth taxi we had previously purchased to get through a down cycle.

Of the three remaining taxis, I kept one to manage on a daily basis and leased out the other two while working as a realtor. Being a director at Co-op, I felt it was only proper that I participate in the taxi business in a hands-on capacity. Although I could have resigned as a director, I served out my term until 1981.

I still did not have an occupation that was truly satisfying, something that was a joy to do. The real estate business was all-consuming, much more so than the taxi business. I was fortunate that I had my family's support, as well as other outlets.

~

In 1983, we bought our first-ever brand new home in a new development in Thornhill, a suburb of Toronto, where our children grew up. My grandmother used to say that even our two hands are different. I have yet to meet anybody whose children are the same, and our two kids were no exception. David, our first-born, is a talented, brooding type with great emotional depth and maturity. Our Kati is a social butterfly with just as much depth and maturity. Both children seem to have a flair for writing. Sadly, neither child possesses robust health. I attribute this to the fact that even the third generation after the Holocaust are afflicted by its horrors. I believe that trauma is passed down through generations.

On June 17, 1984, my son, David, had his bar mitzvah. Had my grandfather lived long enough, I think he would have enjoyed and agreed with the following speech I delivered:

Today you are Bar Mitzvah, a son of the Covenant, a man in the eyes of God and your peers. We are here to celebrate a joyous occasion and an age-old tradition. We have our friends and relatives to share our simcha with us. But it is important that while we celebrate our happiness today, we should remember those who cannot be with us, especially your two grandfathers.

In a cemetery in Hungary stands a monument marking the final resting place of some of the hundreds of thousands who perished in the Holocaust. My father – your grandfather – and a lot of others are buried there. On this monument there is an inscription:

Megölte öket a gyülölet Örizze emléküket a szeretet.

Hatred has killed them, may love cherish their memories.

You represent that love. You are that love. You are a link in a chain – a chain that was nearly broken, but was not! And you are here as living proof of the miracle of life, of Judaism and of tradition.

The famous philosopher George Santayana once said, "Those who do not remember their past are condemned to repeat it." Well, my son, you know your past because as your Bar Mitzvah present your grandparents took you back to Hungary last summer to acquaint you with the origin of your parents' birthplace. They took you back to that cemetery where my family, the family that you never got to know, is resting forever. I believe that is where you passed into manhood, because you showed your heart and your soul. In that far-away cemetery, you shed a tear and you said the traditional prayer for the dead, the Mourner's Kaddish.

The Biggest Fight

My volunteer work with B'nai Brith continued, including writing articles for *The Observer*. As the chair of the Lodge's League for Human Rights, I took my duties seriously. I therefore followed the war crimes trial of Imre Finta, a high-ranking Hungarian police captain in charge of assisting the Nazis in sending Hungarian Jews to the death camps. He was accused of war crimes and his trial was held in Toronto in 1989. As Holocaust survivors from Hungary, my mother and I took special interest in the Finta trial and attended most of the court hearings.

Many people get the impression of the courts and justice system from television; this trial was nothing like it. I had gone to court with a great deal of mixed emotions. I anticipated witnessing history in the making, and I had a specific purpose at the same time: to write a report on my observations. It was most appropriate, an observer for our *Observer*. Little did I know what I would witness.

Upon entering the courtroom, spectators chose their seats according to their affiliations. In the centre were the supporters of the Crown – Jewish groups, visiting students and so forth. On the left were the Finta supporters and on the right were the reporters and media types. Since I was taking notes, I sat on the right.

The questions and answers were at times rambling, unrelenting and all of a sudden brutal and cunning. I would like to convey the sense of these proceedings by explaining how they were conducted. Since the witness was speaking Hungarian, simultaneous translation was provided by two translators. At times, Finta's main lawyer, Doug Christie, gave a hard time even to the translators. The jury members listened through headphones.

Judge Archie Campbell, Crown prosecutor Christopher A. Amerasinghe and defence lawyer Douglas Christie had travelled to Hungary, and other locations, to take testimony under Canadian procedure in a foreign courtroom. The witness was cross-examined and questioned in exactly the same manner as if the trial was happening in Canada. The whole testimony was videotaped and played in front of the jury and the audience in Toronto.

One videotaped testimony was that of a most extraordinary ninety-year-old witness, Béla Liebman. Mr. Liebman had been a sergeant in the Austro-Hungarian Army during World War I and had been awarded the highest possible honour, the German Iron Cross. He survived the Holocaust in a forced labour camp and was able to return to Szeged in January 1945, at which time the Soviets had already liberated the city and were in charge of it.

Mr. Liebman was an accredited photojournalist, and the Soviets ordered him to take pictures of the ghetto, synagogues and surrounding areas of Szeged. Eventually his pictures were placed in the national archives of Hungary and all his pictures and originals were authenticated.

Now, you've got to picture a ninety-year-old man cross-examined on the witness stand by a relentless, brutal and rude lawyer tormenting and badgering a witness who was a survivor. The scene is very hard to describe, yet throughout the whole procedure, this was when I felt the most reassured. Looking at Béla Liebman, I felt strangely at ease. His face was sad, intelligent, articulate and without emotion. With his glasses perched on his nose, it was almost as if he was a patient teacher giving instruction to an unruly student about human dignity. And dignified he was. In this one courtroom scene I was able to take in the enormity of the crime and the answer to it – dignity, the human spirit and our right to life. This man calmly answered the same question again and again, regardless of how many times he was asked. He never lost his temper or raised his voice.

When Christie asked Mr. Liebman to describe the photo that he had taken of the remnants of the Szeged ghetto, Mr. Liebman had to explain where the ghetto building ended and the ghetto fence started. Patiently, he tried to explain to Christie that this would be impossible, because the wall had been destroyed and only remnants of the fence remained standing.

This video segment lasted for a long time. During the showing of this video, Christie was looking on from his chair with a toothpick in his mouth and laughing out loud. Sabina Citron, a survivor who founded the Holocaust Remembrance Association, had walked out in disgust and shortly after, the rest of the group I was with did the same. We were all angry and shocked.

I was so incensed by the way the trial was conducted that I composed two letters of complaint right then – one protesting the way Liebman had been badgered as a witness and another expressing my frustration at Christie's behaviour in court. Five other supporters signed the letters. I did not expect a reply to my letters, but I received one from the Department of Justice, stating that copies of my letters had been forwarded to Mr. Justice Campbell and to Mr. Douglas Christie, defence counsel. I had not expected my letter to have consequences, but I was tremendously pleased when it did. Unfortunately, I was not in court when it happened, but Christie made reference to this letter, even asking for a mistrial. He said that during his years as a lawyer he had never received anything like it and he felt threatened by it! The mistrial was, of course, denied, but he grabbed any excuse to get a mistrial on numerous occasions before and after this incident. He gave a feeble explanation of his behaviour, claiming that he'd remembered something funny, unrelated to the trial. I don't think anybody bought it; I certainly didn't. However, from this point on, the judge did not allow Christie the leeway that he had previously enjoyed with regard to his questioning and, in fact, Christie was warned a number of times about his behaviour. Not allowing Christie his theatrics was a bit of a turning point in the trial.

During most of the trial, the accused, Imre Finta, appeared to be asleep, as if he had seen this movie and knew the ending. My mother was in the courtroom the day Judge A. Campbell gave his instructions to the jury, who found Finta innocent of all charges. The reaction from the witnesses and survivors who were present at the announcement of the verdict were all the same: "These people don't understand! They couldn't possibly comprehend!" The Crown appealed the decision twice, once to the Supreme Court, which upheld the decision in 1994. I did not believe that justice had been served.

$\sim$

Two years later, in 1991, I discovered a lump in my throat. Magdi insisted I go to see the doctor, even though I'd recently had a checkup. Once again, Magdi was right. The lump was a malignant tumour. Magdi and my mother were beside themselves; David and Kati were at a loss as to how to deal with the situation.

I considered the cancer to be a temporary illness, just one more challenge, admittedly a big one. I was so convinced that I would be all right that I just threw myself into all my activities. The day before the operation, I even played racquetball for one and a half hours.

Just a short while before my illness struck, a wonderful group of people, under the leadership of Rabbi Berg from New York, set up the first Kabbalah Centre in Toronto. The organization is devoted to exposing the wonders of Judaism to those interested in learning why we do certain things in Judaism. Magdi was one of the centre's first students, and I was the real estate agent who negotiated the offer to purchase the group's home in Toronto, a combination synagogue and study centre.

When we learned I had cancer, Magdi requested that all the Kabbalah study centres in the world participate in a communal prayer service on my behalf. In Jewish tradition, the prayer in solitude is less powerful than the communal prayer. I am convinced that the prayers of Magdi, my mother, David and Kati, along with the members of all the Kabbalah centres in the world, were heard by God and my martyred father and grandparents, whom I believed were watching over me. Once again, I was not alone in my fight.

When it was confirmed that I had thyroid cancer, considered to be a slow-spreading disease, I was booked to see a specialist in three months' time. We didn't know that the disease had already spread to my vocal cords and two of my lymph nodes. When our friend from the Kabbalah Centre, Dr. Auby Kurtz, found out about the long wait, he arranged for Dr. Rosen at Mount Sinai Hospital to operate on me almost immediately. Dr. Rosen was not only a specialist in thyroid cases, but a man with golden hands. It took two operations within a month of each other, but he saved my life and my voice. Being in reasonably good physical condition, having the support of family and friends and focusing on my work all helped to speed my recovery.

After my two operations in November and December of 1991, I had to go for radiation therapy and frequent checkups. However, a mistake was made in my aftercare, and I wasn't given a medication I needed until three months after the surgery. One serious effect was the loss of my strength. I did not even have enough strength to go up the stairs in our home. Due to the lack of medication, I also ballooned by twenty-five pounds. On sheer willpower alone, I made an offer presentation two weeks after my surgery, but it wasn't the same as before. I had lost my feel for real estate. I was suffering complete mental and physical burnout.

In my frame of mind, the long evening hours and weekend work connected with the real estate business seemed overwhelming. Even before my cancer diagnosis, I had been finding the business increasingly difficult. My physical weakness only exacerbated the problem. It was time to change direction yet again. I decided that I did not want to work in real estate any longer. Magdi, my ever-loving and supportive wife, was with me all the way. There was only one technical difficulty: I was grown up, fifty years old, so what was I going to do? There was one thing that Magdi and my mother begged me not to do: drive a cab. I did drive my cab, but for just a few weeks. I wanted to make sure that I still had the taxi blood circulating in my veins.

Everything happens in its own good time. Because I wanted a change from driving a taxi, I went into the real estate business, and because of the nature of the real estate business, I returned to the taxi industry. On my return, I found myself in a brand new position, doing something that I had never considered before: I became an industry advocate, researcher, analyst and sales manager at Co-op Cabs. My real estate training was the foundation for all these activities.

A customer service department did not exist at any of the taxi companies at the time. I advocated for Co-op's need to hire an individual with sales training to focus on customer service. It took almost a year (which I needed anyway for my full recovery), but the eight directors were finally convinced of the need for such a position and believed that I was the right person for the job. In 1993, I became Co-op's Manager of Sales and Customer Service. A red and yellow company car with the customer service logo on its side was at my disposal.

I am very proud of the fact that due to my intervention, the Wheel-Trans contract – transporting people who are elderly or disabled – was awarded to the taxi industry of Toronto, including Co-op Cabs. The Toronto Transit Commission had been ready to award the multimillion-dollar contract to private, unlicensed carriers. This large contract helped all cab companies, especially the smaller ones, which couldn't have survived otherwise during those tough economic times. I spent up to 30 per cent of my Co-op time on taxi industry issues at the commission and at City Hall, and I spent more than ten years as a volunteer spokesperson and advocate for the taxi industry.

Making a Difference Together

After my mother's book was first published in 1990, she started to receive invitations to give public presentations about her book and her experiences during the war. In 1993, totally unbeknownst to us, Professor Marlene Kadar of York University in Toronto began to use my mother's book in her Life-Writing course. In June of that year, my mother told me that she had been invited to the last class and wanted me to accompany her. Of course I agreed, but I was puzzled about the reason for my presence. She was told that since the book was about me as well, the class wanted to meet both of us. There were twenty-five to thirty students present. As we were entering the room, Professor Kadar said, "Here come Ibi and Professor Réti." My mother asked me about my title, and I said I would explain later.

My mother was presented with a bouquet of flowers, and some refreshments were served. We participated in a wonderful question-and-answer period with the students and Professor Kadar. The students then lined up to get my mother to autograph their copy of her book. I was so proud of my mother!

And here is how I came to be called Professor Réti: In early 1993, my phone had rung. The young woman on the line identified herself as Denise Bain, a student in Professor Kadar's class, and said that she would like an interview. When I informed her that my mother was not living with me, she said that she and another student, Ian McKay, would like to talk with me. I was intrigued and agreed to a meeting.

On the appointed day, Denise and Ian explained to me that their assignment was to write about one of the books in their course, and they had chosen my mother's. They wanted to take a different approach by interviewing me. Like my mother, who never missed an opportunity to talk about me, her son, I talked about my children during the interview. I said that as a parent, I considered it my duty to teach my children about life. I wanted to emphasize that if I could teach them how to think for themselves, then I was doing a good job. In my enthusiasm, I referred to my experiences as being the equivalent of a PhD in Life. Obviously this statement was later discussed in class, because that was the only way Professor Kadar could have had knowledge of it. It was very satisfying to know that our stories and, most importantly, my mother's experience, were making a difference.

To my great pleasure, the lecture at York University about my mother's book became an annual event to which my mother and I were always invited. In the spring of 2002, there were more than 250 students in the lecture hall at York University learning about my mother's story. I realized that Professor Marlene Kadar was helping to stamp out ignorance and racial intolerance, which sadly still exist in our world today. She was opening the eyes and minds of numerous young people to the past, the present and the future. And my mother and I were a part of this process.

The following article I wrote was published in the *Observer* in 1996 and expresses some of my feelings about the book, my mother, the lecture and Professor Kadar:

UNIVERSITY STUDENT FOR A DAY

It was an odd feeling sitting in a large lecture hall surrounded by over two hundred young students, listening to the professor and taking notes just like all others. Sitting between my mother and my son just height-ened the feeling.

The date is March 13, 1996. The place is York University in Toronto. The topic is Life Writing and antisemitism in Hungary. The lecturer is Professor Marlene Kadar. The background reading material is my mother's book, An Ordinary Woman in Extraordinary Times.

Professor Kadar invited my mother and her family to attend the lec-ture. She wanted to surprise her class at the end of the lecture by intro-ducing the author of the book. Believe me, she did surprise them! She succeeded beyond anybody's imagination!

Professor Kadar began by posing a few questions. This was the first time that I noticed that everybody had a copy of the book. Judging from the students' answers, it was apparent that some (but not all) had read the book and were familiar with its contents and subjects.

"Who is Ibi Grossman and why did we choose her book? What is ex-traordinary about her ordinariness? What is the significance of being a Holocaust survivor, single mother, Jewish identity, escapes, adapting to a new country, lack of language?" All good questions, I thought.

Imagine my feeling – our lives as a subject of a university lecture! However, the odd feeling was still lingering. I couldn't describe it. As the lecture was progressing, I couldn't help my mind wandering a little. I was thinking how different our lives would have been had my father also survived. Had he lived, had he not been murdered for the sole rea-son of being a Jew! Our lives were literally an open book in front of these young people. There was a lingering image in my mind, a picture on the front page of Time *magazine. It was a photograph taken about two years ago. The picture showed a group of men who were all skin and bones, standing behind a barbed wire fence. The picture was taken at a modern-day concentration camp, the result of the Bosnia-Serbia con-flict. Another concentration camp, and only a mere fifty years after the Holocaust. Is that how my father looked at the end? Why was he forced to be part of a madman's "final solution" to a non-existing problem?*

Why? Why? Why?

I am an adult now. I have lived with this question all my life. I grew up with it. The men in the picture were somebody's father, husband, son or brother. They were fellow human beings subjected to inhuman cruelty. They were punished for the same "crime" for which my father was murdered – the jailed men had a different religion from their tormentors. This time the process was called "ethnic cleansing." My God! Have we not learned anything during the last fifty years? Does history really repeat itself?

As I continued listening to Professor Kadar, my odd feeling began to dissipate. I was beginning to feel better. At the end of the lecture, there were about fifty students lining up to get my mother to autograph her book. Some of the kids had tears in their eyes. I am very proud of my mother, who made it possible for me to be a university student for a day and a student of history for life. I am also very grateful to Professor Kadar, an extraordinary teacher, who invited us.

My mother was invited to several other places to talk about her Holocaust experiences, including Toronto's Holocaust Education and Memorial Centre, where she had at first been a volunteer docent since 1986, when it opened. After a few years, she became a regular Survivor Speaker there.

In 1991, on Yom HaShoah, Holocaust Remembrance Day, I spoke during the candle-lighting ceremony at Baycrest Terrace, to both residents and community members. I read the following "Acceptance" from a collection of writings that were read at one of the concluding ceremonies of the World Gathering of Holocaust Survivors in the United States, an event that began in the early 1980s.

THE ACCEPTANCE

We accept the obligation of this legacy. We are the first generation born after the darkness. Through our parents' memories, words and silence, we are linked to that annihilated Jewish existence whose echoes permeate our consciousness. We dedicate this pledge to you, our parents, who suffered and survived; to our grandparents, who perished in the flames; to our vanished brothers and sisters, more than one million Jewish children, so brutally murdered; to all six million, whose unyielding spiritual and physical resistance, even in the camps and ghettos, exemplifies our people's commitment to life.

We pledge to remember. We shall teach our children to preserve forever that uprooted Jewish spirit, which could not be destroyed. We shall tell the world of the depths to which humanity can sink, and the heights which were attained, even in hell itself. We shall fight antisemitism and all forms of racial hatred by our dedication to freedom throughout the world.

~

In 1998, in honour of Israel's fiftieth birthday and as a tribute to my mother's admirable example, I also became a docent at the Holocaust Centre. My duties consisted of guiding visitors for the two-hour tour, providing a brief background on the Holocaust, explaining the exhibits, fielding questions and introducing the Survivor Speaker. I was the only docent at the centre who was a survivor and worked together with a parent. My mother was immensely proud that we were the only mother-and-son team, both survivors.

The first time I accompanied my mother was to a presentation to Grade 6 students. I listened as she referred to her baby, whom she was trying to save from starvation. She also related an incident when she hid her wedding band in her baby's diaper. In the front row, a little girl was listening with rapt attention. At the end of the speech, this girl was the first to ask questions. She wanted to know, "Where is your baby now?" I was standing at the back of the room and without hesitation my mother pointed to me and said, "You see that middle-aged man? That is my baby." The next question was the turning point. The student wanted to know where the wedding band was that she had hid inside the diaper. The ring in question was the wedding ring that my father had given her. My mother was so determined to save that ring that she took the exceptional step of hiding it rather than handing it over to her captors.

My mother was wearing the wedding ring that Emil had given her, and explained to the girl that she kept her original wedding band at home. After the presentation, we went to lunch and discussed the event. I suggested she put the original ring on her necklace and show it to the students in all future presentations, and that is exactly what she did.

Epilogue

My mother's last presentation was in October of 2004. Five months later, when I had the horrible task of clearing out her apartment after her death, I came upon her necklace with the ring on it. I decided to make the ring into a showpiece, which I would wear only when at the Holocaust Centre and on special occasions. I call it the Ring of Love. The ring was ready in April of 2005, and the first special occasion took place on May 5, 2005, through the Jewish Motorcycle Alliance. It was the first ever Ride To Remember (R2R), which commemorates the Holocaust. The official theme was "We ride to remember, so the world will not forget." I had loved motorcycles since riding one on my eighth birthday, and I now equate riding with freedom. Three years earlier, I had joined a Jewish motorcycle club called Yids (Jews) on Wheels (yow).

On the Ride to Remember, we rode to Washington, DC, to meet up with 250 other bikers and visit the US Holocaust Memorial Museum. Since the ring was too big to wear under my riding glove, I had kept it inside my breast pocket during the ride. One particular scenic curve held my attention longer than the law of physics permits, and I crashed. When you crash a motorcycle doing sixty, usually either the bike gets banged up, or you do. Not this time – I was riding with the ring of love close to my heart. I feel that, through this ring, my mother is with me at each motorcycle rally, and at each stop I display her picture and story on my bike.

In May 2012, our R2R was held in Toronto and Ottawa. I had the honour of reciting the following pledge on the steps of Parliament Hill. Since then, the pledge is an integral part of each presentation I make.

My name is Andy Réti, a young child Holocaust survivor and a member of the YOW motorcycle club of Toronto. Less than seventy years ago, the world of six million Jewish people, including my own father, came to an end in an act that is so evil, that the only word that can describe it is Holocaust.

*I stand before you as a witness and a free man, to tell all: **Never Again!***

***Never Again** to any and all genocides!*

***Never Again** to racial hatred!*

***Never Again** to a second Holocaust!*

*Please take this pledge by repeating it with me. We pledge to speak up against hatred and racism. We pledge to remember. Please put your hand over your heart and say, We pledge – **Never Again!***

Five years earlier, I had become a full-time survivor speaker, literally following in my mother's footsteps by telling our stories at Toronto's Holocaust Centre, schools and libraries in the Greater Toronto Area. In 2013, I joined the Simon Wiesenthal Centre to give even more presentations to students. I am proud to say that I have had the opportunity to tell our story to thousands of people, most of them young students. As part of my presentation I thank my audience in helping me to honour my mother by listening to our story. My presentation includes a PowerPoint titled "The Ring of Love" that focuses on my mother's wedding band, which I wear at each presentation, and I include photos and a two-minute video clip spoken by Ibi herself. The questions posed to me and letters I receive are proof and validation of our message: education overcomes ignorance and love trumps hate.

I tell my audience that every Holocaust survivor story is a love story – a love of life, love of family and love of freedom. My extraordinary mother exemplified these ideals. I consider it my duty and legacy to tell our stories to future generations to ensure that we will never again have another Holocaust. As a survivor speaker, I tell each group that one of the lessons of the past is to speak up when we witness something wrong. All my life, I spoke up because of my background. I am convinced that the only way to eliminate prejudice, hate and ignorance is to teach understanding and tolerance. I am proud that I am able to teach these principles and ideals to so many young people. I am equally pleased to have the opportunity to encourage them to appreciate life, the greatest gift of all.

Glossary

Arrow Cross Party (in Hungarian, Nyilaskeresztes Párt – Hungarista Mozgalom; abbreviation, Nyilas) A Hungarian nationalistic and antisemitic party founded by Ferenc Szálasi in 1935 under the name the Party of National Will. With the full support of Nazi Germany, the newly renamed Arrow Cross Party ran in Hungary's 1939 election and won 25 per cent of the vote. The party was banned shortly after the elections, but was legalized again in March 1944 when Germany occupied Hungary. Under Nazi approval, the party assumed control of Hungary from October 15, 1944, to March 1945, led by Szálasi under the name the Government of National Unity. The Arrow Cross regime was particularly brutal toward Jews – during their short period of rule they murdered approximately 20,000 Jews, many of whom had been forced into the Budapest ghetto at the end of November 1944. *See also* Szálasi, Ferenc.

Auschwitz (German; in Polish, Oświęcim) A town in southern Poland approximately forty kilometres from Krakow, it is also the name of the largest complex of Nazi concentration camps that were built nearby. The Auschwitz complex contained three main camps: Auschwitz I, a slave labour camp built in May 1940; Auschwitz II-Birkenau, a death camp built in early 1942; and Auschwitz-Monowitz, a slave labour camp built in October 1942. In 1941, Auschwitz I was a testing site for usage of the lethal gas

Zyklon B as a method of mass killing, which then went into wide usage. Between 1942 and 1944, transports arrived at Auschwitz-Birkenau from almost every country in Europe – hundreds of thousands from both Poland and Hungary, and thousands from France, the Netherlands, Greece, Slovakia, Bohemia and Moravia, Yugoslavia, Belgium, Italy and Norway. Between May 15 and July 8, 1944, approximately 435,000 Hungarian Jews were deported to Auschwitz. As well, more than 30,000 people were deported there from other concentration camps. It is estimated that 1.1 million people were murdered in Auschwitz; approximately 950,000 were Jewish; 74,000 Polish; 21,000 Roma; 15,000 Soviet prisoners of war; and 10,000–15,000 other nationalities. The Auschwitz complex was liberated by the Soviet army in January 1945.

bar mitzvah (Hebrew; pl. b'nai mitzvah; literally, one to whom commandments apply) The time when, in Jewish tradition, children become religiously and morally responsible for their actions and are considered adults for the purpose of synagogue and other rituals. Traditionally this occurs at age thirteen for boys and twelve for girls. Historically, girls were not included in this ritual until the latter half of the twentieth century, when liberal Jews instituted an equivalent ceremony and celebration for girls called a bat mitzvah. A bar/bat mitzvah marks the attainment of adulthood by a ceremony during which the boy/girl is called upon to read a portion of the Torah and recite the prescribed prayers in a public prayer service.

B'nai Brith (Hebrew; literally, children of the covenant) An international mutual aid organization that was founded in New York in 1843 to fight antisemitism and support human rights. B'nai Brith advocates on behalf of Jewish communities and also offers a variety of services for families and seniors. Members form groups called lodges to provide social programming and volunteer-based community services. The Canadian arm, founded in 1875, is headquartered in Toronto, with branches in other cities.

British Mandate Palestine The area of the Middle East under British rule from 1923 to 1948, as established by the League of Nations after World War I. During that time, the United Kingdom severely restricted Jewish immigration. The Mandate area encompassed present-day Israel, Jordan, the West Bank and the Gaza Strip.

Budapest ghetto The area established by the government of Hungary on November 29, 1944. By December 10, the ghetto and its 33,000 Jewish inhabitants were sealed off from the rest of the city. At the end of December, Jews who had previously held "protected" status (many by the Swedish government) were moved into the ghetto and the number of residents increased to 55,000; by January 1945, the number had reached 70,000. The ghetto was overcrowded and lacked sufficient food, water and sanitation. Supplies dwindled and conditions worsened during the Soviet siege of Budapest and thousands died of starvation and disease. Soviet forces liberated the ghetto on January 18, 1945. *See also* ghetto.

Canadian Jewish Congress (CJC) An advocacy organization and lobbying group for the Canadian Jewish community that existed from 1919 to 2011. The CJC was restructured in 2007 and its functions subsumed under the Centre for Israel and Jewish Affairs (CIJA) in 2011.

Communist Party of Hungary First founded in 1918 and resurrected in 1945 following the liberation and occupation of Hungary by the Soviet Union. The Party was assisted both openly and clandestinely by the USSR and initially had the support of many Hungarians who had opposed the wartime pro-Nazi government in Hungary. The Communist Party merged with the Social Democratic Party in 1948 and was renamed the Hungarian Socialist Workers' Party; it consolidated total power in Hungary by 1949, which it held until 1989.

displaced persons People who find themselves homeless and stateless at the end of a war. Following World War II, millions of people, especially European Jews, found that they had no homes to return to or that it was unsafe to do so. To resolve the staggering refugee crisis that resulted, Allied authorities and the United Nations Relief and Rehabilitation Administration (UNRRA) established Displaced Persons (DP) camps to provide temporary shelter and assistance to refugees, and help them transition towards resettlement.

Finta, Imre (1911–2003) The first person in Canada to be charged with war crimes and crimes against humanity. In the spring of 1944, Finta, a captain in the Hungarian Gendarmerie, the police force, participated in the detention and forced deportation of 8,617 Jews in Szeged, Hungary. Finta immigrated to Canada in 1948, settled in Toronto in 1953, and was charged in 1987. His acquittal by jury in 1990 was appealed, but the appeals were dismissed by both the Ontario Court of Appeal and the Supreme Court of Canada, which accepted his defence of following orders. The Finta trial effectively ended war crimes trials in Canada, with the federal government subsequently choosing to seek to revoke the Canadian citizenship of alleged war criminals, and attempt to deport them.

ghetto A confined residential area for Jews. The term originated in Venice, Italy, in 1516 with a law requiring all Jews to live on a segregated, gated island known as Ghetto Nuovo. Throughout the Middle Ages in Europe, Jews were often forcibly confined to gated Jewish neighbourhoods. During the Holocaust, the Nazis forced Jews to live in crowded and unsanitary conditions in rundown districts of cities and towns.

High Holidays (also High Holy Days) The autumn holidays that mark the beginning of the Jewish year and that include Rosh Hashanah (New Year) and Yom Kippur (Day of Atonement). Rosh Hashanah is observed with synagogue services where the leader of the service blows the shofar (ram's horn), and festive meals where sweet foods, such as apples and honey, are eaten to symbolize and celebrate a sweet new year. Yom Kippur, a day of fasting and prayer at synagogue, follows ten days later. *See also* Yom Kippur.

Horthy, Miklós (1868–1957) The Regent of Hungary during the inter-war period and for much of World War II. Horthy presided over a government that was aligned with the Axis powers and support-ed Nazi ideology. After the German army occupied Hungary in March 1944, Horthy served primarily as a figurehead to the pro-Nazi government; nevertheless, he was able to order the suspen-sion of the deportation of Hungarian Jews to death camps in the beginning of July 1944. Horthy planned to withdraw his country from the war on October 15, 1944, but the Nazis supported an Ar-row Cross coup that same day and forced Horthy to abdicate.

Hungarian Revolution (1956) A spontaneous uprising against the Soviet-backed Communist government of Hungary in October 1956, the Hungarian Revolution led to the brief establishment of a reformist government under Prime Minister Imre Nagy. The rev-olution was swiftly crushed by the Soviet invasion of November 1956, during which thousands of civilians were killed.

Iron Curtain A term coined by Sir Winston Churchill in 1946 to de-scribe the metaphorical boundary that physically and ideologi-cally divided Europe into two separate spheres of influence at the end of World War II: one in Eastern Europe, controlled politically, militarily and economically by the Soviet Union; the second in Western Europe, allied with Western liberal democracies, eco-nomically predisposed to market economics and under the mili-tary protection of the United States.

Jewish Colonization Association (JCA) A Paris-based philanthropic organization founded in 1891 by Baron Maurice de Hirsch that helped establish credit facilities and agricultural training cen-tres internationally. During the 1920s the organization focused on helping Jews immigrate to Canada, Argentina and Brazil. In 1927, JCA merged with two other aid associations to create a suc-cessor agency, HICEM, which continued to help Jewish refugees with immigration. In Canada, the JCA's work was overseen by the Jewish Agricultural Society of New York until a Canadian branch was created in November 1906 that helped Russian Jews settle in agricultural colonies in Manitoba and Saskatchewan. While these colonies were dissolved by the mid-1940s because of economic factors, land purchases and loans to Jewish farmers in Quebec and Ontario continued until 1970. The Canadian committee of the JCA ceased functioning in 1978.

Jewish Congress The Hungarian Department of the World Jewish Congress, which opened in March 1946, engaged in legal and political activities to have confiscated property returned to Hungarian survivors, collected statistical data to better understand the losses and needs of the Jewish communities, collected historical documentation of the persecution of Jews, and supported and educated orphaned children by opening the Louise Wise Home for Children in Budapest in July 1946. *See also* World Jewish Congress; Louise Wise Home for Children.

Jewish houses (Budapest) Also known as "yellow star" buildings (*sárga csillagos házak*). Designated buildings marked with a yellow Star of David that the Nazis ordered the Jews in Budapest to move into in June 1944, three months after Germany occupied Hungary. More than 200,000 Jews were assigned to fewer than two thousand apartments. They were allowed to leave the buildings for two hours in the afternoon, but only if they wore an identifying yellow Star of David on their clothing. This meant they could be easily located when the time came for them to be deported. *See also* ghetto; yellow star.

Kabbalah (Hebrew; literally, received) An area of study in Judaism that deals with mysticism and meditation.

kibbutz (Hebrew) A collectively owned farm or settlement in Israel, democratically governed by its members.

kosher (Hebrew) Fit to eat according to Jewish dietary laws. Observant Jews follow a system of rules known as *kashruth* that regulates what can be eaten, how food is prepared and how animals and poultry are slaughtered. Food is kosher when it has been deemed fit for consumption according to this system of rules. Several foods are forbidden, most notably pork products and shellfish.

landsmen (Yiddish; in English, hometown societies) Groups of Jewish immigrants from the same towns, cities or regions in eastern and central Europe. In North America, Jewish immigrants often joined these organizations for support and a social network.

Lichtenwörth A town in eastern Austria that was the site of a forced labour camp – as part of the Mauthausen concentration camp complex – during World War II. In December 1944, approximately 2,500 Hungarian Jewish women were sent on a death march from Budapest to Lichtenwörth. Those who survived the march were subjected to slave labour in inhumane conditions, causing an unknown number of deaths.

Louise Wise Home for Children An orphanage that was opened in Budapest on July 28, 1946. In 1948 it was taken over and operated by the American Jewish Joint Distribution Committee, a humanitarian aid organization. The orphanage was named after Louise Waterman Wise (1874–1947), a prominent American philanthropist who began working with children living in New York slums in the 1890s, went on to create a national child adoption agency in 1916 and assisted, through the American Jewish Congress, Jewish refugees as they fled Europe in the 1930s.

Mengele, Josef (1911–1979) The most notorious of about thirty SS garrison physicians in Auschwitz, Mengele was stationed at the camp from May 1943 to January 1945. One of the camp doctors responsible for deciding which prisoners were fit for slave labour and which were to be immediately sent to the gas chambers, Mengele was also known for conducting sadistic experiments on Jewish and Roma prisoners, especially twins.

moshav (Hebrew; literally, settlement or village) An agricultural cooperative comprised of individually-owned farms that was founded by the Labour Zionist movement in the early twentieth century.

Radio Free Europe (RFE) A radio network that began operating in

July 1950 to provide an independent, uncensored source of news and analysis to countries that lack a free press. Its first broadcast was from a studio in New York to then-communist Czechoslovakia. RFE currently broadcasts in twenty-eight languages to twenty-three countries.

Roma Also known as Romani. An ethnic group primarily located in central and eastern Europe. The Roma were commonly referred to as Gypsies in the past, a term now generally considered to be derogatory, and they have often lived on the fringes of society and been subject to persecution.

Sabbath (in Hebrew, Shabbat) The weekly day of rest beginning Friday at sunset and ending Saturday at nightfall, ushered in by the lighting of candles on Friday evening and the recitation of blessings over wine and challah (egg bread); a day of celebration as well as prayer, it is customary to eat three festive meals, attend synagogue services and refrain from doing any work or travelling.

Schmidhuber, Gerhard (1894–1945) A German general who commanded German army forces in Hungary in 1944. Schmidhuber is remembered for indirectly negotiating with Swedish diplomat Raoul Wallenberg, which resulted in the prevention of the destruction of the Budapest ghetto. *See also* Wallenberg, Raoul.

shmatte (Yiddish; literally, rag) A term sometimes used to refer to clothing.

shtetl (Yiddish) Small town. A small village or town with a predominantly Jewish population that existed before World War II in Central and Eastern Europe, where life revolved around Judaism and Judaic culture. In the Middle Ages, Jews were not allowed to own land, and so the shtetl developed as a refuge for Jews.

Siege of Budapest The battle from December 24, 1944, to February 13, 1945, between German and pro-German Hungarian troops and the Soviet Red Army and Romanian army; the latter encircled Budapest to liberate the city. The Hungarian and German armies surrendered on February 13.

Stalin, Joseph (1878–1953) The leader of the Soviet Union from 1924 until his death in 1953. Born Joseph Vissarionovich Dzhugashvili, he changed his name to Stalin (literally, man of steel) in 1903. Very soon after acquiring leadership of the Communist Party, Stalin ousted rivals, killed opponents in purges, and effectively established himself as a dictator. During the late 1930s, Stalin commenced "The Great Purge," during which he targeted and disposed of elements within the Communist Party that he deemed to be a threat to the stability of the Soviet Union. These purges extended to both military and civilian society, and millions of people were incarcerated or exiled to harsh labour camps. During the war and in the immediate post-war period, many Jews in Poland viewed Stalin as the leader of the country that liberated them and saved them from death at the hands of the Nazis. At the time, many people were unaware of the extent of Stalin's own murderous policies. After World War II, Stalin set up Communist governments controlled by Moscow in many Eastern European states bordering and close to the USSR, and instituted antisemitic campaigns and purges.

Szálasi, Ferenc (1897–1946) The founder and leader of the Hungarian fascist Arrow Cross Party, which actively collaborated with the Nazis in Hungary, notably in the persecution and deportation of Jews. Szálasi was convicted of war crimes and executed in 1946. *See also* Arrow Cross Party.

Torah (Hebrew) The Five Books of Moses (the first five books of the Bible), also called the Pentateuch. The Torah is the core of Jewish scripture, traditionally believed to have been given to Moses on Mount Sinai. In Christianity it is referred to as the "Old Testament."

tzaddik (Hebrew, from a root word meaning justice; also spelled *tsaddik*) A holy, righteous person.

Wallenberg, Raoul (1912–1947?) The Swedish diplomat who was sent to Hungary in June 1944 by the US Refugee Board and succeeded in saving tens of thousands of Budapest Jews by issuing them Swedish certificates of protection. The Swedish government also authorized Wallenberg to set up thirty "safe houses" and organize food distribution, medical assistance and child care for Jews in Budapest. Of the slightly more than 100,000 Jews that remained alive in Budapest at the end of the war (out of a pre-war population of 247,000), the majority were saved through his efforts. Wallenberg was awarded the title of Righteous Among the Nations by Yad Vashem in 1986 and has been honoured by memorials or monuments in ten other countries.

World Jewish Congress An international advocacy organization established in Geneva, Switzerland, in 1936 to fight the rising persecution of Jews in Europe. Its precursors were the American Jewish Congress and France's Comité des Délégations Juives. The congress currently represents Jewish communities in one hundred countries and is engaged in seeking adequate compensation for Holocaust survivors, in interfaith dialogue and in combatting antisemitism, among other issues.

yarmulke (Yiddish; in Hebrew, *kippah*) A small head covering worn by Jewish men as a sign of reverence for God.

yellow star (Star of David; in Hebrew, *Magen David*) The six-pointed star that is the ancient and most recognizable symbol of Judaism. During World War II, Jews in Nazi-occupied areas were frequently forced to wear a badge or armband with the Star of David on it as an identifying mark of their lesser status and to single them out as targets for persecution.

Yom Kippur (Hebrew; literally, Day of Atonement) A solemn day of fasting and repentance that comes eight days after Rosh Hashanah, the Jewish New Year, and marks the end of the High Holidays. *See also* High Holidays.

Photographs

1 Ibolya (Ibi) Szalai with her parents and two of her sisters. From left to right: Ibi's sister Elizabeth; her mother, Laura; her sister Aranka; her father, Ignácz; and Ibi. Pécs, Hungary, 1921.

2 Ibi's older sisters, Margaret (left) and Ilona (right), 1920.

3 Ignácz and Laura Szalai. Pécs, Hungary, 1942.

1 Ibi (second from the left) with her friends in the Zionist group, 1933.
2 Ibi and her husband, Zoltán, 1939.

Ibi and her son, András (Andy), after the war. Budapest, 1947.

1 Zolti's parents, Henrik and Janka Réti, with Ibi and Andy after the Holocaust. Budapest, 1946.

2 Ibi with her two sisters who survived the Holocaust. In the back row: Ibi (left) and Elizabeth (right); in front, Aranka. Budapest, 1950.

3 Andy's 8th birthday gift – a motorcycle ride on the outskirts of Budapest, 1950.

Andy and Ibi, 1953.

1 Ibi and Andy in the year after arriving at their first destination in Canada. Winnipeg, 1957.
2 Andy wearing his "new" naval overcoat in front of Central Tech. Toronto, 1958.
3 Ibi and Emil's wedding. Toronto, December 14, 1958.
4 Andy (second from the left) reuniting with his friends from Bezerédy elementary school. Left to right: Mike (Miklós), Andy, Irwin (Ervin) and Julius (Gyuszi), Toronto, 1959.

1 Reunion with Ibi's sister Elizabeth soon after her family's arrival in Toronto, 1960. Back row, left to right: Elizabeth, Aranka and Ibi. In front, left to right: Elizabeth's son, Tomi; Aranka's daughter, Marianna; and Andy.

2 Andy and his mother, Ibi, at Zoltán's memorial in Budapest, Hungary, 1974.

1 Andy and Magdi's wedding. From left to right: Ibi's husband, Emil; Magdi (Magdalene) Vadnai; Andy; and Andy's mother, Ibi. Toronto, December 15, 1968.
2 Andy with the first cab he owned, 1969.

1

2

1 Andy and Magdi with their children, Kati and David, at a B'nai Brith Lodge picnic, circa 1983.

2 Celebrating the bar mitzvah of Andy's son, David, with all of Andy's remaining
family. Toronto, 1984.

1 Ibolya Grossman signing her books at the launch of *An Ordinary Woman in Extraordinary Times*. Toronto, 1990.

2 At the Holocaust Centre in Toronto, by the plaques commemorating her parents and her husband, Zolti, 1991.

1 Ibi wearing her first wedding ring, 2001.
2 Andy and Ibi at the book launch of *The Son of an Extraordinary Woman*, 2002.
3 Ibi on her birthday, 2002.

1 Andy (third from the right) on the Ride to Remember. Washington, DC, 2005.
2 The photos and story of his mother that Andy displays on his motorbike during stops on the Ride to Remember. New York, 2007.

The Ring of Love, which Andy wears during presentations to students and on special occasions. Western Wall, Jerusalem, 2008.

1 Andy and Judy's wedding, 2006. Standing in back, left to right: Andy's son, David; Judy; Andy; Judy's son Evan; and Judy's son Jeremy. Seated in front, left to right: Andy's aunt Elizabeth; Andy's aunt Aranka; Judy's mother, Edith; and Jeremy's wife, Voula.

2 Wedding of Andy's son, David, to Stephanie. From left to right: Evan, Jeremy, Voula, Judy, Stephanie, David, Andy, Andy's daughter, Kathy, and Kathy's husband, Darryl. May 2013.

1

2

3

4

1 Andy holding his portrait and certificate of recognition in front of his mother's portrait and story in the "We Who Survived" gallery at the Neuberger Holocaust Centre. Toronto, 2015.

2 Andy and Judy with family in the "We Who Survived" gallery. From left to right: Andy's daughter, Kathy; his son-in-law, Darryl; Judy's daughter-in-law, Voula; Judy's son Jeremy; Andy; Judy's son Evan; and Judy.

3 Andy's granddaughters, Leah (left) and Tara (right).

4 Judy's granddaughters, Andrea (left) and Eliana.

Andy and his wife, Judy, 2014.

Index

The Azrieli Foundation

The Azrieli Foundation was established in 1989 to realize and extend the philanthropic vision of David J. Azrieli, C.M., C.Q., M.Arch. The Foundation's mission is to support a wide spectrum of initiatives in education and research. The Azrieli Foundation is an active supporter of programs in the fields of Education, the education of architects, scientific and medical research, and the arts. The Azrieli Foundation's many initiatives include: the Holocaust Survivor Memoirs Program, which collects, preserves, publishes and distributes the written memoirs of survivors in Canada; the Azrieli Institute for Educational Empowerment, an innovative program successfully working to keep at-risk youth in school; the Azrieli Fellows Program, which promotes academic excellence and leadership on the graduate level at Israeli universities; the Azrieli Music Project, which celebrates and fosters the creation of high-quality new Jewish orchestral music; and the Azrieli Neurodevelopmental Research Program, which supports advanced research on neurodevelopmental disorders, particularly Fragile X and Autism Spectrum Disorders.